The Authors

Maralene and Miles Wesner are multi-talented teachers and prolific writers. They have published more than 150 Audio-Visual Education aids, and pioneered new reading methods with their Phonics in a Nutshell (1965).

They have written articles, and mission studies for Southern Baptist periodicals. They were in the original group of writers to develop WMU's Big "A" Club material.

They've published several books with Broadman Press: *A Fresh Look at the Gospel* (1983); *You Are What You Choose* (1984); and *How To Be a Saint When You Feel Like a Sinner* (1986) and self-published 30 books by Diversity Press.

They are noted for their no-nonsense style, their clear illustrations, and their willingness to face controversial issues. From the dual perspectives of both academic and religious professions, they seek to be a bridge between the spiritual and the intellectual worlds.

They hold Masters Degrees (MEd) from Oklahoma University plus work toward a Doctorate. Miles also attended Southwestern Baptist Theological Seminary, and served as a high school counselor. He has been the bi-vocational pastor of a small rural church for more than 50 years.

Both Maralene and Miles taught in public school and collages and served as educational consultants. Maralene taught Psychology and Speech for Southeastern Oklahoma State University for 32 years. She was chosen Oklahoma Teacher of the Year in 1975.

They have planned, led tours, and done research in all of the 50 states, Canada, Mexico, Europe, Egypt, Japan, and the Holy Land.

In 1985, they were among a small group of Americans who were invited by Dr. Joseph P. Kennedy of the US/China Education Foundation and Bishop Ting, leader of the Three Self Movement, to participate in the First Symposium on the Church in Nanjing, China.

Now, they use their lifetime of varied experiences to write insightful sermons, essays, and books.

Titles by Maralene & Miles Wesner
published by Nurturing Faith

Sermons for Special Days

Life More Abundant

Do You Really Know Jesus?

If Jesus Were Here Today

101 Sparks of Inspiration

When God Can't Answer

Think (Or Else!)

Stumbling to Zion

Sensible Sermons

Finding Truth in the Parables

The Unknown God

Truth or Tradition?

Maralene & Miles Wesner

Seven *Difficult* Doctrines

Reinterpretations to Bring Hope
Instead of Harm

© 2025
Published in the United States by Nurturing Faith, Macon, GA.
Nurturing Faith is a book imprint of Good Faith Media (goodfaithmedia.org).
Library of Congress Cataloging-in-Publication Data is available.

ISBN:978-1-63528-260-3

All rights reserved. Printed in the United States of America.

Scripture quotations are from New Revised Standard Version Bible, copyright 1989, Division of Christian Education of the National Council of the Churches of Christ in the United States of America. Used by permission. All rights reserved.

Contents

Foreword by John D. Pierce 1

Rationale 3

Introduction 7

1. Reinterpreting the Doctrine of Scriptural Inerrancy 13

2. Reinterpreting the Doctrine of Divine Sovereignty 25

3. Reinterpreting the Doctrine of the Trinity 37

4. Reinterpreting the Doctrine of the Vicarious Atonement 47

5. Reinterpreting the Doctrine of Supernatural Miracles 61

6. Reinterpreting the Doctrine of a Literal Hell 73

7. Reinterpreting the Doctrine of a Physical Second Coming 83

Conclusion 93

Foreword

By John D. Pierce

Prophetic words are not easy to hear but needed in order to get on track. That was true in biblical times and remains so today.

In our current setting, however, we have too few voices willing to speak truth passionately, critically and clearly.

Miles and Maralene Wesner have long assumed that important prophetic role. They have been speaking and writing such timely and needed words for decades. We are fortunate to hear from them again.

This book continues their important mission with perhaps even more boldness. It is only when confronting what is being done wrong that one has the knowledge and capacity to do what is right.

Longtime educators, authors and ministers, the Wesners communicate clearly that the right way for those who profess to be Christians is the way Jesus called all of his followers to live.

"The experiences of these last few years prove that our current religious teachings have been totally ineffective," Maralene wrote plainly in a recent blog. "Both churches and schools have failed miserably in preparing people to live in a world filled with scam artists, propaganda experts and false information."

She noted that Jesus warned his followers of such gullibility and waywardness and called for spiritual discernment rather than being easy targets.

In this book, the Wesners point to seven particular doctrines as being widely misinterpreted and misleading for masses of professing

Christians. By digging into these doctrines, they separate assumptions and off-track conclusions about the Bible from biblical truth.

To be a critic is to analyze something carefully. The Wesners are much-needed, loyal critics of the Christian faith.

They show how so many purveyors and adherents of Americanized Christianity have strayed from a primary commitment to reflecting the life and teachings of Jesus to affirming poorly conceived doctrines and embracing contrasting and controlling ideologies.

Wise readers will hear and consider these warnings with open minds and hearts. Even better, is a willingness to replace misguided understandings with the ones that are more in line with Jesus' example and calling.

These well-articulated, scholarly yet pastoral critiques do not simply demolish some long-held beliefs. They offer better, more hopeful understandings of how God has reached into humanity through Jesus and given us a way to live more effectively and abundantly on this side of eternity.

God bless the Wesners for continuing to give us the best of their minds and hearts — so that we can be more thoughtful and loving followers of Jesus.

> —John D. Pierce, retired editor of *Nurturing Faith Journal* and current director of the Jesus Worldview Initiative through Belmont University's Rev. Charlie Curb Center for Faith Leadership

Rationale

Traditional Christianity simply didn't work for us, even though we were dedicated and faithful for many years. As lifelong Southern Baptists from daily Bible-reading homes, we participated in Sunday school, morning worship, Training Union, Sunday night services, Wednesday prayer meetings, Vacation Bible School, and annual revivals.

We attended a denominational university, entered the ministry, tithed, worked in large and small churches, directed music programs in evangelistic crusades, and were utterly miserable. Far from being led astray by liberals, we begged for any ray of light and couldn't see anything different in churches or colleges. We couldn't even buy books with enlightening views in Christian bookstores.

Totally isolated in the rural Bible Belt, we struggled alone. Finally, after decades of searching, we began to find a few life-saving writings outside of our denomination and often outside of Christianity itself. Even these, however, tended to be almost useless. Those that were readable seemed shallow, and those that contained profound concepts were couched in obtuse language. We feel compelled, therefore, to share some of our spiritual insights, using simple, everyday terms.

We are not opposed to these basic doctrines just to be different or rebellious. Rather, we challenge them because we have seen the damage they can do. If we follow them to their logical conclusions, we soon realize how inhumane and unproductive they can be.

Christianity has at least seven difficult doctrines that often hinder it from being accepted by thinking people:

1. *Scriptural inerrancy* is an impossible doctrine because words and language don't have exact meanings. Furthermore, it forces us to believe

that snakes talk, that God killed babies in every Egyptian household, and that God told parents to have their young sons stoned to death if they were rebellious. These and many more ridiculous statements and commands are found in the Bible.

2. *Divine sovereignty* sounds like a good doctrine, but it won't stand scrutiny. If God causes everything that happens, then miscarriages, birth defects, and evil and senseless acts are God's fault.

3. *The Trinity* is a confusing doctrine. It tries to combine a spiritual God with Jesus, who is half-God and half-human. We know God and Jesus are separate because Jesus says, "Your will, not mine, be done." Then it adds a strange creature who seems to stir emotions and affect language. These three entities operating as one can't be explained in a reasonable manner.

4. *The vicarious atonement* is obviously a pagan notion based on the idea that the gods can be influenced by good odors and blood offerings. That is why children and virgins were sacrificed in many religions. If such bribes and payments are required for salvation, then God isn't wise or good, and grace is certainly not a gift.

5. *Supernatural miracles* are fragments of primitive superstitions. They attempted to explain things like weather and natural disasters because science and natural laws were not understood. But it's hard to convince modern people that donkeys talk, that the sun stands still, that God made a woman from a man's rib and then changed another woman into a salt statue.

6. *A literal hell* is a horrible doctrine because it depicts a divine being cruel enough to inflict punishment for which no person or beast has ever advocated. Civilized countries forbid the torturing of people today. Even Hitler didn't impose eternal suffering. That is vengeance at its worst; it achieves nothing and perpetuates evil forever.

7. *A physical second coming* is a detrimental doctrine because every generation thinks they will be either rescued or destroyed during their lifetime. No future is possible, and any progress is futile. Why would we

work to protect our planet from pollution or climate change if we expect a cataclysmic event any day? This belief destroys all human initiative.

In general, these teachings encourage passive acceptance when we desperately need active achievement. They validate fantasy when we desperately need reality. They increase prejudice when we desperately need acceptance. They stymie intellectual growth when we desperately need wisdom. They waste time on trivial matters when we desperately need profound understanding. They offer temporary palliatives when we desperately need permanent cures.

Above all, they present a God who is cruel and fickle when we desperately need a God who is loving and truthful. That is why we must reinterpret these doctrines if our faith is to influence intelligent individuals or even survive in this modern world.

Introduction

An out-of-town stranger once stopped an old mountaineer and asked, "Hey, fellow, does this highway lead back to town?"

"Well, no, not exactly," the mountaineer replied. "You see, it's like this. That highway goes over the hill and turns into a road. Then the road moseys along for a piece and turns into a path. The path continues a little farther and turns into a pig trail. That pig trail finally become a squirrel track. The squirrel track runs into a scrub oak and ends up slap-dab in a knothole!"

Many religions are like that. Many beliefs are like that. Many doctrines are like that. They may look promising at the beginning. They may be attractive on the surface. They may be useful for the short term. But if you follow them blindly, you'll eventually end up "slap-dab in a knothole."

Do our doctrines glorify God? Do they reflect God's truth, righteousness, and love? Do they make God look good? If they don't, they're wrong.

In fact, the God of the early scriptures operated on questionable standards. God punished people who had been deceived (e.g., Gen 12:17). God was less humane than Moses and had to be reminded of God's promises (e.g., Exod 32:9–14). God revealed malicious prejudice against wounded people and innocent illegitimate children (e.g., Deut 23:2). God ordered strangers killed if they came near the worship site (e.g., Num 3:10). Some verses even state that God killed or commanded others to kill babies and children (e.g., Exod 12:29; Lev 26:22; Deut 2:33–34; Isa 13:16; Hos 13:16). Yet Jesus's attitude toward children was very different (e.g., Matt 18:6).

It is obvious that God—as the original, omnipotent creator—could have ordained whatever rules God desired. Therefore, when we describe total depravity or the vicarious atonement or eternal perdition, we're actually saying, "That's the way God wanted things to be!" We're saying that out of all God's possible options, God chose to set up these ridiculous systems. We must not simply accept and perpetuate such traditional dogmas.

As intelligent Christians we must examine every belief. Jesus said, "Beware that no one leads you astray" (Matt 24:4).

We must try every spirit. John said, "Do not believe every spirit, but test the spirits to see whether they are from God" (1 John 4:1).

We must follow every theological teaching to its ultimate conclusion in order to understand what kind of result it produces. If a doctrine tends to produce bad fruit, questionable results, and perverted behavior, then it's not valid.

Jesus told us we can recognize valid teachings by their effects: "Every good tree bears good fruit, but the bad tree bears bad fruit. A good tree cannot bear bad fruit, nor can a bad tree bear good fruit" (Matt 7:17–18).

That is why we must make tentative projections to see what the consequences would be if a given ideology was put into practice universally, if a given philosophy was adhered to constantly, and if a given system was embraced completely. We must ask ourselves, "If everyone in the world accepted this precept literally and lived by this precept absolutely, would civilization be strengthened or weakened?" If we honestly have to conclude that the overall effect would be destructive, then that precept is not valid, no matter how many professing Christians believe it.

We need to realize that some of these beliefs evolved at a time when they fulfilled special needs. We know this because if they had not helped certain people or answered certain questions or solved certain problems, they never would have survived. However, when new discoveries were made and deeper levels of understanding were reached, the old beliefs should have been reexamined and either reaffirmed, adapted, or discarded as the situation warranted.

Unfortunately, by the time the change was needed and the reexamination occurred, most of these beliefs had already become well-entrenched dogmas. Once they had settled into rigid creeds and rituals, the pressures of tradition and custom enabled them to live long beyond their usefulness.

There is a need to accept the fact that as human beings we don't have absolute truth. We're searching and growing. We're learning by trial and error. Therefore, if something serves a purpose for a while and then becomes unworkable, obsolete, or irrelevant, we should feel free to replace it or reinterpret it.

A God of truth and righteousness and love would never decree false principles. Such a God would never want us to cling to that which serves no purpose. God would never want us to propagate things that hinder our development. God would never want us to use processes that block the kingdom's progress. In short, if a belief or a practice is not productive, if it doesn't bear good fruit, it's not to be considered of God.

Furthermore, just because a certain belief is the best one available at a given moment, that doesn't mean it can't be revised at some later date. The language a two-year-old uses may be appropriate for him or her, but we certainly expect it to change and improve as he or she matures. The interests of teenagers may be perfectly appropriate for them, but we certainly expect them to change and broaden as they mature.

Why can't we be this sensible in viewing religious doctrines? We must allow for spiritual development. A belief that served well in a first-century Roman age or a sixteenth-century Puritan age may be totally counterproductive in a twenty-first-century computer age.

Maybe the doctrine was productive for them. Maybe it was the best they could formulate. Maybe it helped them cope with life's complexities. Maybe it gave partial answers to disturbing questions. Maybe it provided tentative solutions to perplexing problems.

But things change! To insist upon perpetuating doctrine indefinitely is detrimental and ludicrous. We don't make a person wear the same shoes at age forty that he wore comfortably at age four. Why should we, in our more technological and humane society. be forced to accept conclusions from people in primitive times? At some early date, did God say, "That's it! I've spoken my last word on every subject!" If inerrancy is true, then the last words were spoken centuries ago.

Before his crucifixion Jesus said, "I still have many things to say to you, but you cannot bear them now. When the Spirit of truth comes, he will guide you into all the truth, for he will not speak on his own but will speak whatever he hears, and he will declare to you the things that are to come" (John 16:12–13)

It is true that some axioms are immutable and unshakable. These, however, can be summed up in a few words. Jesus expressed them this way: "'You shall love the Lord your God with all your heart and with all your soul and with all your mind.' This is the greatest and first commandment. And a second is like it: 'You shall love your neighbor as yourself.' On these two commandments hang all the Law and the Prophets" (Matt 22:37–40).

That's everything we are really sure of! Beyond these two bedrock absolutes lies a whole world of ambiguities that must be studied and handled as we grow and develop. How we show our respect for God in worship can be varied. How we minister to others can be adapted. How we describe our own spiritual insights can be revised. This is what makes the gospel living water.

Jesus didn't say, "My message is a stagnant pool that will never change." He said, "My message is alive! It's fresh and flowing and able to quench your thirst" (see John 4:10–14).

We must eliminate or reinterpret beliefs and practices that nullify Christian teachings.

Jesus believed in evaluating the evidence. He judged things by the results they produced. Therefore, we must look at the fruit of our doctrines. For instance, the doctrine of scriptural inerrancy often produces bad fruit. "You shall not permit a [witch] to live" has instigated enormous tragedies (Exod 22:18). In 1484 the Pope ordered witches to be burned. From 1515 to 1516 over five hundred women were killed by Protestants. The Salem witch trials in America bore witness to another deadly example.

A superstitious belief in demons leads to dangerous and destructive exorcisms. Because of such ideas, mentally ill people have been persecuted, and babies have been beaten to death.

Even emphasizing the innocent-sounding trait of submission can justify prejudice, discrimination, and domestic violence, as well as unfair treatment in matters of gender and race. Advocating corporal punishment increases child abuse and never aids in discipline.

Teachings about divine sovereignty often leave the impression that if God is absolutely in charge, then God can prevent evil but chooses not to. That's wrong!

A doctrine of the Trinity that views God, Jesus, and the Holy Spirit as three entities is misleading and confusing. Instead, they reflect three steps of spiritual development. In the beginning, people worshiped a God "out there." Then they saw God reflected in Jesus. At last, after Pentecost, they believed God could be in ordinary human beings as the Holy Spirit.

The doctrine of vicarious atonement presents the unreasonable concept of depravity. Teaching that every individual is sinful enough to be worthy of eternal punishment does great damage to self-esteem. That's dangerous because we live up to or down to our perception of self-worth.

When we destroy one's self-image, we create many psychological problems. This doctrine gets entangled with sacrificial customs and other confusing ideas. It also encourages believers to label and judge others.

A belief in supernatural miracles leads to bad fruit. Depending on such events causes disillusionment and resentment when they don't occur as expected. Someone said, "An occasional win is the worst thing that can happen to a gambler because it sets him up for addiction and ultimate failure." It's the same with miracles. Furthermore, they tend to distract us from deeper issues. For instance, many people only know that a snake talked to Adam and Eve, that Lot's wife became a pillar of salt, and that Moses parted the Red Sea. They completely miss any moral lessons in these accounts.

Jesus repudiated people who desired signs and dramatic incidents (e.g., Mark 8:12).

The doctrine of a literal hell validates our worst traits of vindictiveness and revenge. It also portrays a cruel God and creates fear and unhealthy emotions.

A belief in the physical second coming prevents any long-term progress. It is bad fruit because it discourages education and hinders conservation efforts relating to pollution and climate change. It can even promote fanaticism. In 1999 one group prepared a plot to shoot police and stage an Armageddon battle in order to hasten Jesus's return.

Jesus was practical and sensible. He was ruthless about ignorance and waste. He said trees that don't produce good fruit should be cut down (e.g., Luke 13:7).

He would encourage us to reinterpret any beliefs and doctrines that are obviously contrasting and damaging to the gospel. An absolute mindset concerning theology has prevented the ongoing changes and adaptations we should have been making over the years. As a result we have built up a backlog of problems.

Evaluating the effect of doctrinal positions on personal progress is hard. How can we tell if a principle is valid? How can we tell if a process is constructive? How can we tell if a path is a potential highway or a potential pig trail? In short, how can we tell if the life we are leading and the faith we are propagating are going to end up in a knothole?

We need to be sure that our beliefs reflect a moral God who can help us develop ethical characters. Our beliefs should concern ultimate questions of universal significance rather than superficial trivialities. They should make us more tolerant and inclusive, and they should further all civilization in a positive, progressive manner.

As responsible Christians we must face facts. None of us wants to waste our lives and resources in a bankrupt system. None of us wants to pour our talents down the drain. In short, none of us wants to end up in a knothole.

Therefore, doctrines that are detrimental and destructive must be reinterpreted.

Chapter 1

Reinterpreting the Doctrine of Scriptural Inerrancy

The stones containing the divine oracles were carefully sealed in alabaster jars. Each stone was covered with innumerable tiny marks that were considered to be sacred. These words of the gods were inscribed with precision. Every rule was engraved. Every ritual was ordained. Every requirement was proscribed. Indeed, everything a person would ever need to know about life was there, just waiting to be decoded. Since each bit of hieroglyphics had only one absolute definition and each pictophrase had only one absolute meaning, no uncertainty was possible. Clear instructions were provided for every potential contingency. Any individual in a quandary about personal choices or proper ceremonies or public morals had only to open the jar, find the right stone, transcribe the particular marks, and he would know exactly what to do! Every dilemma had been anticipated. No new problems could ever develop. No new situations could ever arise. No new information would ever be needed. No interpretation was necessary. No allowance was made for mitigating circumstances. No adaptation or change was tolerated. All things were truly written in stone. "Thus saith the gods" could not be questioned. The oracles were inerrant and infallible!

How simple! How reliable! How ridiculous!

Scriptural inerrancy must be reexamined. Most misconceptions could be cleared up if we understood how the scriptures developed. These sacred writings didn't fall out of heaven in one neat package. The Bible contains many manuscripts and fragments of manuscripts. As they were compiled over the years, some had missing pieces, and some overlapped. For instance, most people don't know that 2 Kings 19 and Isaiah 37 are identical. Why would God dictate these same passages twice?

When the amount of written material had increased and accumulated, in the fourth century CE a group of religious leaders met to decide which documents should be included and which should be excluded. There were serious differences of opinion. Many apocalyptic writings were left out of the canon, yet several of these had been in general use when Paul declared that "all scripture is inspired by God" (2 Tim 3:16).

In fact, there was no Bible as we know it when Paul made that often-quoted statement. Contrary to popular belief, Paul didn't say, "The Bible is inspired by God." He didn't say, "The Hebrew prophecies are inspired by God." Instead, he said, "All writings are inspired by God." Since very little written material was available, people respected and revered it.

Jude even quotes two of these nonbiblical sources. Once, he described how the archangel Michael disputed with the devil about the body of Moses (see Jude 9). He told how Enoch prophesied that the Lord is coming with thousands upon thousands of his holy ones (see Jude 14).

Joshua also quotes from a book of Jashar, which is not included in our Bible, saying, "The sun stood still, and the moon stopped" (Josh 10:13).

So how do we know the "right" manuscripts—and only the right manuscripts—got included in our present Bible?

Words aren't precise and static. Of course, God's word or truth is absolutely inerrant and infallible. But that word isn't written down anywhere. Truth is a perfect concept in the mind of God. The moment it's reduced to human phrases and sentences, it becomes fallible. That's because vocabulary and grammar are human inventions of this world and, thus, subject to imperfection. No idea can be perfect, except in its nonverbal stage, because language simply is not an inerrant vehicle.

When a concept is put into linguistic form, it immediately becomes imprecise. Even such a simple word as *dog* evokes as many impressions as there are hearers. Some think of their pet. Others may think of a rabid animal. Furthermore, in translation, synonyms aren't exact, and idioms can't be paralleled. For instance, one person said, "Man, you look cool." Another one said, "Man, you don't look so hot." Now, the literal meaning of *cool* and *not so hot* is almost identical, but the real meaning of these two statements is totally opposite.

Cultural changes also affect language. *Gay* doesn't mean the same thing now as it did in the 1920s. When a group of people heard the word *Blondie* on TV, older individuals immediately thought of the comic character, Dagwood Bumstead's wife. Younger individuals thought of a music group. Now, which was right? You can't answer that question! Both could be right, or neither could be right. So was that word inerrant and infallible? Of course not! No word is!

Ancient Hebrews had little knowledge about science and biology. They knew nothing of genes or DNA, so early writers tried to explain natural phenomena (e.g., Gen 30:37–39). They also had a lot of taboos (e.g., Lev 17:10–11). They were superstitious about death (e.g., Num 19:11). Some procedures were cruel as well as ignorant (e.g., Num 5:16–27).

They had many strange commands: "You shall not sow your vineyard with two kinds of seed, or the whole yield will be forbidden, both the crop that you have sown and the yield of the vineyard itself. You shall not plow with an ox and a donkey yoked together. You shall not wear clothes made of wool and linen woven together" (Deut 22:9–11).

If a wise and loving God planned to compile one special book of instructions for his followers, he'd make every word count. He'd omit empty, trivial matters. He'd avoid contradictory commandments. He'd delete any confusing statements. He'd certainly never recommend violence or vicious revenge.

Unfortunately, a lot of the material in the Old Testament and some in the New Testament does include unimportant, irrelevant details concerning genealogies and obsolete issues. The ancient writers gave pedantic descriptions of priests' clothing (see Deut 22:12). There are also mundane requirements for sacrificial procedures and endless admonitions about forbidden foods.

If God was truly preparing a once-and-for-all moral document and personally breathing all of the crucial information that readers would desperately need in the future, why would he waste so much time and space on things that would not be useful to later generations? If this was to be the sacred, inerrant treatise that people would label as "holy" and be willing to die for, then it should contain only the best and highest spiritual advice, and that advice should be expressed in the clearest and most efficient way possible. It's obvious that the canonized Bible we have today is not such a book!

Also, why do we assume the group of old men who later assembled the final manuscript, deciding what to include and what to exclude, were any more inspired than current scholars and researchers?

If Christianity and salvation were going to be explained perfectly with words that are dictated directly from the mind of God, then why on earth didn't Jesus tell his disciples about this tremendously significant project? He didn't even mention it! He never said, "I'll be leaving a book of infallible written instructions for your benefit. You must study it and faithfully follow its teachings." Instead, he promised them something much better: "When the Spirit of truth comes, he will guide you into all the truth, for he will not speak on his own but will speak whatever he hears, and he will declare to you the things that are to come" (John 16:13).

It's strange that Christians revere and indeed almost worship the written version of these words from God but ignore and neglect the spiritual version that each of us has within us.

Why did the doctrine of scriptural inerrancy develop?

In the early days, writing was rare, and manuscripts were scarce. Therefore, anything that was considered important enough to be preserved in script was taken very seriously. Also, primitive men and women depended on priests and kings to define their behavior. Democracy was unthinkable, and autonomy was unknown. Most human beings, even today, seem to need concrete guidelines. Rules and regulations written down in black and white are more influential than verbal suggestions. That's probably because children learn to rely on external supervision. Their attitudes are shaped and actions are curbed by authority figures. Therefore, even when they are adults, they find it difficult to make crucial decisions without the security of a predetermined correct response.

Nevertheless, flexibility is necessary. Most decisions involve a mixture of ethical elements. The breaking of one good principle may enable us to keep another better principle. For example, in Nazi Germany, if the Gestapo questioned someone about harboring a Jew, should he be truthful and allow them to take the victim to a gas chamber, or should he lie and protect him? This type of moral dilemma requires analytical thought and a lot of uncertainty.

Most people don't like to think. That's why believing they have definite answers in the Bible about everything is reassuring.

What problems occur as a result of the doctrine of scriptural inerrancy?

The fixation with infallibility has many drawbacks. In the first place, life is complex, ambiguous, and fluid. It doesn't stand still and lend itself to rule-keeping. Trying to adhere to an absolute moral code makes for a rigid, guilt-ridden lifestyle.

Distorted understanding of scriptures encourages ignorance and stifles growth. When you explain that a particular verse is being used out of context or is at odds with other verses, determined literalists always retort, "But the Bible says!" They don't realize the level of maturity, the cultural situation, and symbolic figures of speech must all be taken into consideration. We need to remember that reason is a God-given attribute that shouldn't be abandoned during Bible study.

Also, we are not told when this supernatural perfect knowledge descended. Was it present during the long-term thought and organization process or only during the actual act of writing? Paul was certainly not aware of his infallible inspiration: "We know only in part…but when the complete comes, the partial will come to an end…. Now I know only in part; then I will know fully, even as I have been fully known" (1 Cor 13:9, 12).

Even if inerrant original autographs were possible, they would only have reached a few people. The very moment another generation arose or another language group became involved, the problem would reappear. Why, if infallibility is so essential, didn't an omnipotent God breathe each language translation with the same precision? Isn't it just as important for later generations and other nationalities to be protected from error as it was for those first Hebrews and Greeks? Such speculations become endless and illogical.

God wouldn't be a respecter of persons if he gave a few ancient writers access to absolute truth while forcing the rest of us to struggle through second-hand and third-hand communication barriers.

Interscriptural conflicts are also common. One verse says, "Moses and Aaron…and seventy of the elders of Israel went up, and they saw the God of Israel…. They beheld God, and they ate and drank" (Exod 24:9–11). Later, God says, "No one shall see me and live" (Exod 33:20).

The scriptures expressly forbid Moabite descendants from entering the worship area (see Deut 23:3), yet David, a direct Moabite descendent (only three generations removed), is described by God as "a man after my heart" (Acts 13:22).

In Genesis, God seems to change his mind: "The LORD was sorry that he had made humans on the earth" (6:6). Yet in Malachi, God says, "I the LORD do not change" (3:6).

Trying to reconcile verses from different writers and places and times and circumstances is impossible. If we must look for a Bible verse every time we try to make a decision, we'll fail to develop our own moral standards.

Some scriptures support discrimination. Many statements degrade women (e.g., Lev 15:19–21). Women were once considered property (e.g., Deut 21:10–12). Paul even blamed women for original sin (see 1 Tim 2:14).

Unbelievably harsh sentences were prescribed: "If a man has a stubborn and rebellious son who will not obey his father and mother… they shall say to the elders of his town, 'This son of ours is stubborn and rebellious…. He will not obey us.'… Then all the men of his town shall stone him to death" (Deut 21:18–21).

Anyone who deviated from "normal" was condemned (e.g., Deut 23:1).

Religious diversity was a death sentence: "Whoever sacrifices to any god other than the LORD alone shall be devoted to destruction" (Exod 22:20).

Certain political promises have caused Middle Eastern wars. The scripture says, "I will set your borders from the Red Sea to the sea of the Philistines and from the wilderness to the Euphrates, for I will hand over to you the inhabitants of the land, and you shall drive them out before you" (Exod 23:31).

Many scriptures hinder scientific and social movements. From civil rights to women's equality, literalists have hindered social progress. A verse citing mentality has too often condoned religious persecution. It has often fostered offbeat fallacies concerning race, intermarriage, ordination of women, and divorce.

Basing behavior on isolated verses of scripture has caused much pain. For instance, "You shall not permit a [witch] to live" (Exod 22:18) led to the infamous Salem witch trials. "Those who spare the rod hate their children" (Prov 13:24) has caused child abuse. "Slaves, obey your earthly masters with respect and trembling" (Eph 6:5) was used to justify slavery. "Women should be silent in the churches. For they are not permitted to speak but should be subordinate" (1 Cor 14:34) is used to keep women out of leadership roles. "Wives, be subject to your husbands as to the Lord" (Eph 5:22) encourages spousal abuse.

One passage says, "I warn everyone who hears the words of the prophecy of this book: if anyone adds to them, God will add to that person the plagues described in this book; if anyone takes away from the words of this book of prophecy, God will take away from that person's share in the tree of life" (Rev 22:18–19). This threat has caused people to reject new translations, but originally it was added as a curse designed to get certain manuscripts through superstitious Roman censors.

Many scriptures deal with superficial trivialities rather than ultimate questions of universal significance. This encourages hypocrisy since all precepts aren't followed with the same degree of dedicated exactness. Isolated passages are used to persecute biologists who teach evolution and exclude women from ministry, yet other equally plain injunctions are evaded or ignored. For instance, the early church practiced communal living (e.g., Acts 2:44–45). We don't do that today!

Jesus said, "Sell what you own, and give the money to the poor" (Mark 10:21). That command is ignored! No one insists "six days shall work be done" means a five-day work week is sinful (Exod 31:15). Such picking and choosing undermines credibility.

Groups differ over the proper mode of baptism, and each can quote scripture verses to support their view. Some groups use this scripture: "I will sprinkle clean water on you, and you shall be clean" (Ezek 36:25). Other groups use this scripture: "We were buried with him by baptism" (Rom 6:4).

Denominations differ on women's dress (e.g., 1 Cor 11:5). Some illogically require women to wear hats in church and yet won't let them pray or prophesy in public.

Many promises are totally unreasonable: "You shall be the most blessed of peoples, with neither sterility nor barrenness among you or your livestock. The LORD will turn away from you every illness" (Deut 7:14–15). Yet Paul said, "I am content with weaknesses…hardships" (2 Cor 12:10).

Other verses, taken literally, have caused destructive practices and even death (e.g., Mark 16:18).

A human type of God is portrayed in many places: "[The man and his wife] heard the sound of the LORD God walking in the garden" (Gen 3:8). Yet Jesus said, "God is spirit" (John 4:24).

Some scriptures suggest God is too weak to overthrow iron chariots (see Judg 1:19). Another writer suggests God couldn't kill a man (see Exod 4:24). One writer believed God could be shamed into responding favorably (see Num 14:14–16).

Many passages reflect a God of such indefensible conduct that we have to justify or apologize for his actions. In fact, we must either be willing to worship an immoral deity or be willing to give up our verbal inerrancy security blanket.

Supposedly, God even did evil: "Whithersoever they went out, the hand of the LORD was against them for evil" (Judg 2:15 KJV).

People were commanded to commit wholesale murder (see Deut 20:16). Cruelty was justified (see Deut 25:11–12).

God is described as vengeful and inhumane (see Num 11:1, 33). One verse even says God hated a person (see Mal 1:3). Yet the New Testament says, "Let us love one another, because love is from God…; God is love" (1 John 4:7–8, 16).

This doctrine of scriptural infallibility must be abandoned. We need a God of moral and ethical character much more than we need an inerrant Bible!

How can we reinterpret the doctrine of scriptural inerrancy?

First, we must realize that revelation is progressive. Early writers still accepted polytheism. The authors of scripture were inspired to write to the best of their ability, but they could only express things at their level of development.

Jesus updated many Old Testament statements. God supposedly said, "I love those who love me" (Prov 8:17), but Jesus disagreed with this, saying, "You have heard that it was said, 'You shall love your neighbor and hate your enemy.' But I say to you: Love your enemies" (Matt 5:43–44).

Moses said, "Show no pity" (Deut 19:21); "anyone who maims another shall suffer the same injury in return: fracture for fracture, eye for eye, tooth for tooth" (Lev 24:19–20). Yet Jesus denied this, saying, "You have heard that it was said, 'An eye for an eye and a tooth for a tooth.' But I say to you: Do not resist an evildoer" (Matt 5:38–39).

Peter said, "Do not repay evil with evil or abuse for abuse, but, on the contrary, repay with a blessing" (1 Peter 3:9). Paul also said, "Do not repay anyone evil for evil" (Rom 12:17).

In fact, Jesus contradicted several "words of the Lord." The law is clear and definite: "Whoever does any work on the Sabbath day shall be put to death" (Exod 31:15). Yet Jesus rejected this notion, saying, "The Sabbath was made for humankind and not humankind for the Sabbath" (Mark 2:27). Once, Jesus even healed a man on the Sabbath (see John 5:11).

Jesus updated attitudes toward the handicapped (see Lev 21:16–20; Luke 14:13). Over and over, we see Jesus trying to nullify the cruel and damaging effect of supposedly inerrant scriptures.

Jesus updated attitudes toward unclean things (see Lev 5:2). He touched women and lepers and sinners. Peter is told by the same God that nothing is unclean (see Acts 10:15).

Jesus updated attitudes toward idols (see Deut 7:26). Paul said, "We know that 'no idol in the world really exists' and that 'there is no God but one'" (1 Cor 8:4).

Washing rituals were changed (see Lev 22:6; Luke 11:38; Mark 7:2–4, 15).

In the Old Testament, God supposedly sent no rain to the wicked (see Deut 11:17). Yet Jesus said, "[God] sends rain on the righteous and on the unrighteous" (Matt 5:45).

According to the Old Testament, adulterers are to be stoned (see Lev 20:10). Even the innocent partner is punished (see Deut 22:21, 23–24). Yet Jesus told the woman caught in adultery to go, saying, "Neither do I condemn you" (John 8:11).

Jesus seemed to consider Moses's words and Old Testament scriptures in a rational way. He obeyed those that were reasonable, positive, and productive; he ignored or repudiated those that were unreasonable, negative, and unproductive. He probably expects us to use this same approach today about obsolete scriptures.

Next, we must also learn to recognize symbolic language. Many people object to such an interpretation, yet Jesus said scripture can be considered in this light (see Matt 11:13–14).

Paul spiritualized words freely, saying, "In him also you were circumcised with a spiritual circumcision, by the removal of the body of the flesh in the circumcision of Christ" (Col 2:11).

Figures of speech must be considered. Our expression *a month of Sundays* doesn't mean an exact time period, yet many people insist that the scriptures—which refer to six days, forty days and forty nights, or a thousand years—must be viewed as mathematically precise. They are not! For example, if Jesus was crucified on Good Friday and arose on Sunday, he was not in the grave for three days and three nights

Hebrews used the term *Armageddon* to mean any intense conflict. Yet some Bible students insist the word must mean a literal geographically oriented future conflagration. Many weird prophecies have arisen concerning this false belief!

Finally, we must understand and emphasize the role of the Holy Spirit. If every Bible disappeared tomorrow, God wouldn't evaporate! Our God is ultimate, and nothing else is, including the Bible. A pen-and-paper revelation is not the highest one. God can bypass imperfect language by communicating soul to soul and heart to heart. He didn't say, "I will put my words on billboards, bumper stickers, posters, or pages of a book." He said, "I will put my laws in their minds and write them on their hearts" (Heb 8:10).

It's significant that Jesus never once said, "Now, of course, I'm going to leave you written instructions. You will be provided with a holy book full of God-breathed words of wisdom."

Fortunately, we don't need to rely on such externals. Christianity can stand on its own inherent merits. It works! Jesus told us that we can either accept and believe theoretical doctrines, or else we can believe the concrete evidence that proves that his life was productive and positive. He said, "Believe me that I am in the Father and the Father is in me, but if you do not, then believe because of the works themselves" (John 14:11).

The old admonitions—"Believe this because the Bible says so!" or "Do it this way because Paul did it this way"—are not valid. In a multicultural world, many people don't view the Bible as the last word or even the first word. To them, it would be just as logical to say, "Believe this because the Koran says so!" or "Do it this way because Socrates did it this way."

Truth must be acknowledged wherever it is found. In matters such as the creation, we must rely on God's truth as revealed in nature and science for the "how" and God's truth as revealed in scripture and theology for the "why." This is the only way to avoid unproductive disputes.

The scripture declares, "The grass withers; the flower fades, but the word of our God will stand forever" (Isa 40:8). God's word does stand forever. Truth is eternal, but nouns and verbs are not! They change with the times, and so must we. A progressive understanding of Scripture will restore intellectual credibility to Christianity. If anything on this earth was complete and perfect, then it would be God.

The doctrine of scriptural inerrancy must be reinterpreted because progressive revelation is evident, language is imprecise, and each receiver and listener is unique and different.

Chapter 2

Reinterpreting the Doctrine of Divine Sovereignty

The ancient monarch had control of all he surveyed. He was the master of all he touched. He wanted total submission from all his subjects. Homage and adoration were required. He would tolerate no threat to his authority. Instant, unqualified obedience was the greatest value. He rewarded obeisance, not autonomy. He desired dependence, not independence. Growth and maturity were not emphasized because this dictator wanted to keep all his underlings at the serf and slave level. He wanted them to have to come to him for every cup of water and every scrap of bread. He wanted people to bow and beg for favors. He wanted personally to dole out each item as it was needed. He never encouraged anyone to fend for himself or learn life's lessons or stand on his own two feet. He feared that if his subjects developed self-reliance, that might somehow threaten his total control. His ego was so fragile that even discussions about his kingdom procedures made him irate. Those who dared to ask questions incurred his instant wrath.

Even though he was a powerful magician who could do whatever he wished, many of his servants lived in misery and starvation. Disease and accidents caused unbelievable hardships. Occasionally he could be persuaded to solve a problem, but more often than not, he ignored the suffering around him. Was such a despot worthy of respect and worship?

The doctrine of divine sovereignty must be reexamined. An age-old theological dilemma deals with this subject: If God is all good, then he must want to abolish evil. If God is all-powerful, then he must be able to abolish evil. So why does evil still exist?

Over and over we hear, "God is in charge!" But is he really in charge? Bad things happen to good people! The Holocaust occurred! Babies die! Drug dealers prosper! Miscarriages and birth defects decimate families! Innocent people suffer! Does God actually control all these things? If a CEO ran a business like that, we'd fire him! We must think before we quote platitudes. In the real world, moral principles, natural processes, and free will all limit God's actions.

Yes, there are things God cannot do! Paul said, "In the hope of eternal life that God, who never lies, promised before the ages began" (Titus 1:2).

Can a king who has sworn to be honest in all matters of state give special favors to his cronies? Of course he can't! It's not a matter of political clout. It's not a matter of personal concern. It's a matter of integrity.

He may be powerful enough to do it. That's not the question. He could give personal favors, or he could remain an honest ruler, but he couldn't do both. Some things are inherently incongruous. Even God cannot be a truthful liar.

Can a king who promises to be totally impartial overlook a crime that his son has committed? Of course he can't. It's not a matter of ability. It's not a matter of fatherly love. It's a matter of fairness. He could overlook the offense, or he could operate as an impartial ruler, but he couldn't do both! Some things are inherently incongruous. Even God cannot cheat fairly.

Believing that I will inevitably suffer the effects of my irresponsible acts doesn't show lack of faith. Instead, it shows more faith. It says, "My God is better than that! My God chooses to exemplify integrity and fairness instead of giving in to immature, selfish demands."

Can a king who is dedicated to uphold human rights force a young man who is over twenty-one to resign from an undesirable organization just because his parents insist? Of course he can't. It's not a matter of public good or private opinion. It's a matter of personal freedom. He could either make the parents happy, or he could respect individual human rights, but he couldn't do both. Some things are inherently incongruous. Even God cannot create a free dictatorship.

Some Christians say, "I believe God is in charge. Those who doubt this are dishonoring God." That's not so! God's ability isn't the question. Personal freedom and universal principles are the questions! Why would God force his will on free moral agents? Why would God break his promise to make us sons and daughters rather than robots? Why would God compel us to love and serve him? That would be another act of tyranny.

Belief that we are in control of this world doesn't dishonor God. Instead, it respects and honors God! It says, "My God is better than that! My God chooses to offer personal freedom instead of imposing an oppressive autocracy!" The psalmist said, "You have given [humankind] dominion over the works of your hands; you have put all things under their feet" (Ps 8:6).

The word *dominion* means to have supreme power over something. So who is really in charge of events in this world, God or man?

It's obvious that God is not manipulating the universe. The earth is our domain (e.g., Ps 115:16; Mark 13:34; Matt 25:14).

God must be faithful! Too much is at stake! If a person breaks the laws of nature or even, through no fault of his own, gets in the way of eternal consequences, he suffers, not because God wills it, but because as a true and immutable divine father, he has no choice. The capricious universe that would result from a God who arbitrarily intervenes between causes and effects would ultimately destroy everything and everybody.

Jesus revealed an intelligent and caring creator. When he said, "The Sabbath was made for humankind and not humankind for the Sabbath" (Mark 2:27), he abolished for all time the idea that rituals, ceremonies, and worship services are things that must be done in order to placate a wrathful God.

Jesus came to show a completely different view of the true God. He describes God as a father in many parables. He assures us that God gives good gifts (see Matt 7:11). He states that God doesn't want anyone to perish (see 2 Peter 3:9). He even uses an analogy of God seeking his lost sheep (see Luke 15:3–6). Then he depicts him as standing ready to welcome prodigal sons with open arms. He also exemplified God's attitude of total mercy and forgiveness in his own treatment of others.

In Jesus's explanation about the purpose of the Sabbath, he was trying to assure us that religion is not an organization or an institution set up by divine decree. It isn't a system that forces people to honor, praise, and offer constant adulation to an egotistical deity. Instead, religion and the Sabbath admonitions were developed to enhance the lives of human beings.

Jesus referred to God as "Father" hundreds of times. In a crisis he even called him *Abba*, which is an intimate and loving term.

From Jesus's first statement about being in his Father's house (Luke 2:49) to his final prayer on the cross when he said, "Father, into your hands I commend my spirit" (Luke 23:46), Jesus referred to God as his parent. Many of his parables compared God to a human parent.

Maybe we should consider what a good father does and what he really wants his children to do. Does a good father want constant praise? No! Does he want a lot of gifts? No! Does he want his sons and daughters to remain dependent and subservient all their lives? No! On the contrary, a wise parent wants his children to grow up, to mature, and to become autonomous and independent. He wants them to be intelligent and knowledgeable. He wants them to be sensible and productive. He wants them to be happy.

Unfortunately, these are not the attributes most religions emphasize. They are not the attributes most religions encourage their members to develop. Instead, most religions encourage their members to display traits of obeisance, submission, and subservience. These are not positive traits. These are the characteristics that cruel masters require of their slaves. They are the characteristics that harsh despots require of their subjects. They are unproductive traits in a democratic world.

Jesus describes some things good fathers do not do. They don't give their children stones or snakes or scorpions (see Luke 11:12). A good father never refuses to forgive and restore fellowship (see Luke 15:22–24). Good fathers don't hurt and abuse their children. The scripture says, "It is not the will of your Father in heaven that one of these little ones should be lost" (Matt 18:14).

All Jesus's analogies and descriptions prove that God is not a tyrannical despot. Instead, he is a loving father.

Why did the doctrine of divine sovereignty develop?

This concept developed in a world of absolute monarchs. That was the only form of government and authority the people knew. Those who worked for the king or pleased the king were rewarded. Those who displeased the king were punished. Therefore, serving God was considered to be of ultimate importance. Paul said, "Do not lack in zeal; be ardent in spirit; serve the Lord" (Rom 12:11).

Since human beings tend to be immature and lazy, the magnetic pull of a benign dictator is hypnotic. Being subservient has its own rewards. If we're a slave, then we are not responsible. We are not accountable. We cannot be censured for failures and calamities. Wanting someone to take care of us and escaping blame are things that most people desire from birth.

The conditioning of childhood makes all of us long for a parental figure to provide for our needs, to protect us from dangers, and to solve all our problems. Moving from immaturity to maturity is a difficult and painful step. The attractiveness of submission lies in the fact that it absolves us of the tension and stress of independence.

What problems occur as a result of the doctrine of divine sovereignty?

It's obvious that in a modern democracy, language about monarchs and subjects, masters and slaves sounds foreign. Also, belief in absolute sovereignty nullifies the concept that God is love. If he is in control of everything, then he is responsible for all the world's problems.

Some Old Testament scriptures insinuate God created evil (see Isa 45:7).

Then, the belief in divine sovereignty tends to reward apathy. By contrast, Jesus always said, "You must act!" He was perturbed when the disciples woke him up to fix the storm (see Matt 8:24–26).

He was especially disturbed when he found that the disciples had been impotent in the face of the suffering epileptic (see Mark 9:14–19). He often demanded, "How long am I going to have to act for you? I am come that you may have abundant life! Now live that life!"

Inertia is life's enemy! Taking the path of least resistance is an ever-present temptation. The perpetuation of the status quo is a powerful force. Staying put, letting things go, and resisting change are universal phenomena. The scriptures constantly advocate action. Moses was commanded to go! Peter was commanded to come! The paralyzed man was commanded to arise! Over and over the deadly sluggishness of apathy is condemned.

The doctrines and beliefs we hold must generate energy and reward initiative. Many Christians tend to overemphasize the "let go, and let God" aspect of Christianity. We are told to "wait on the Lord," but we're also told to "arise thou that sleepest."

The doctrine of the sovereignty of God forces us to deny reality and make excuses when tragedies occur. Recently, an actress lost a baby and then suffered a debilitating stroke. Someone asked about her religious faith. She replied, "I just can't understand it. God must have blinked!"

This isn't as irreverent an observation as you might think. It actually expresses a deep theological problem. Even scriptural writers used similar phrases when they struggled with adversity. The psalmist says, "Rouse yourself! Why do you sleep, O Lord? Awake, do not cast us off forever! Why do you hide your face? Why do you forget our affliction and oppression?" (Ps 44:23–24). On another occasion he says, "Then the Lord awoke as from sleep, like a warrior shouting because of wine" (Ps 78:65–66).

In short, these inspired writers were saying, "God you're sleeping on the job. Quit playing hide and seek with us." Hurting people always ask, "Where is God when I need him? Where is God when senseless evil obliterates the good? Where is God when oppression makes a mockery of justice?" Does he, in fact, occasionally blink, and is that when the unspeakable atrocities of life occur?

The most vital question we face is this: "What kind of God do we worship?" Is he an omnipotent magician who can make miracles at will but has to be persuaded to do so by prayers and bribes? Is he an erratic despot who bestows bountiful blessings for a while and then, just as suddenly, withholds his protection? Is he subject to moods? Do we have to keep him in a good humor? Does he faithfully supervise our every move and then lose interest and look away?

These are important questions. Did God create a discordant universe? Does he use illogical, inconsistent methods? Does he elect certain people for heaven? Does he choose certain races for special favors? Does he demand submissive, gullible obedience? We can't worship such a God. If he created a fragmented universe, he's not intelligent! If he uses inconsistent methods, he's not compassionate! Individuals are told to become "like their God." Jesus said, "Be perfect, therefore, as your heavenly Father is perfect" (Matt 5:48). Therefore, to become more honest and productive, we must develop a better theology.

The belief in an absolutely sovereign God allows us to play the blame game. When children play Hot Potato, each boy or girl hands a bean bag to his neighbor. They do this as quickly as possible, hoping to be rid of it when the music stops. The one left holding the bag is the loser. That's a picture of life. In all areas of work or play, we hastily pass the buck. We delegate the role of responsibility to others. We want it to be out of our hands at those critical moments of evaluation. Few of us are willing to stand firm. A wise man said, "Success has a thousand fathers; failure is an orphan!"

Doctrines and beliefs that advocate an abdication of human responsibility should be suspect. If a teaching insinuates God is responsible for you or the priest is responsible for you, it needs to be reexamined. You won't grow as long as you can pass the buck of personal autonomy to someone else.

We all know life is unfair! Bad things happen to good people, and good things happen to bad people. If God is sovereign, then such situations require excuses. If God is sovereign, then unanswered prayers require denial. We have to fall back on, "God must have a reason" or "We're just not supposed to know!" Yet we are supposed to know. Jesus said, "Nothing is covered up that will not be uncovered and nothing secret that will not become known" (Matt 10:26). He also said, "To you it has been given to know the secrets of the kingdom of heaven" (Matt 13:11).

Too often, people who believe their prayers were specifically answered or their lives were miraculously spared act as if they have a special relationship with God. They tend to look down on the unfortunate ones whose prayers aren't answered or whose lives aren't spared. It's easy to say, "They didn't believe enough" or "They are being punished for their sins." This attitude encourages smug self-righteousness!

We must accept the fact that logical causes and effects determine events. Our creator deals in ordinary processes, not spiritual hocus-pocus! There are no erratic, supranatural intrusions. If God occasionally changes his laws to protect me from the consequences of my mistakes and deliberately refuses to do so in other cases, then he is unfair. If one survives a plane crash and says, "It was God's will for me to escape," then he is insinuating, "It was God's will for all those other people to die."

Now, if I can prevent a death and don't, I am guilty of murder. If God reversed the law of gravity for me, he'd he obligated to do it for everyone. The scripture says, "God shows no partiality" (Acts 10:34).

Belief in absolute sovereignty hinders progress! The old warning "We mustn't play God" has stymied medical discoveries and scientific breakthroughs for centuries. Every new venture is criticized and condemned. Laws are passed to prevent cloning and gene therapy. Furthermore, if we expect God to do it, why should we work so hard to accomplish it?

Belief in absolute sovereignty claims that God sporadically intervenes, but this doesn't lead to permanent progress. People won't make long-term commitments and spend years in study and preparation if they truly believe God is going to fix it or that God has already ordained everything according to a prearranged plan.

Many Old Testament scriptures even depict a God who deliberately hardened people's hearts, thus taking away their free will and right of choice. This God then punished them for their disobedience (see Exod 4:21; Deut 2:30; Josh 11:20)!

Later, Paul expresses this idea quite differently. He was mature enough to realize a moral God doesn't deliberately control our minds. So he said, "The god of this world has blinded the minds of the unbelievers, to keep them from seeing clearly the light of the gospel" (2 Cor 4:4).

Peter also reinforces this, saying, "The Lord is not slow about his promise, as some think of slowness, but is patient with you, not wanting any to perish" (2 Peter 3:9). Divine compassion is better than divine sovereignty.

How can we reinterpret the doctrine of divine sovereignty?

First we must realize that God and nature are not synonymous. The scripture says, "There was a great wind, so strong that it was splitting mountains and breaking rocks in pieces before the LORD, but the LORD was not in the wind, and after the wind an earthquake, but the LORD was not in the earthquake" (1 Kgs 19:11). This was a significant insight! Primitive people assumed the gods periodically came down to throw lightning bolts and fling hailstones. This erroneous idea caused great confusion. Even in the twenty-first century, many insurance companies still call earthquakes, volcanoes, and floods "acts of God." Such catastrophes are not acts of God; they are acts of nature.

When Jesus said, "[God] makes his sun rise on the evil and on the good and sends rain on the righteous and on the unrighteous" (Matt 5:45), he was explaining that God doesn't manipulate weather to punish or reward. Wind and rain and storms and volcanoes and earthquakes simply constitute a normal part of the dynamics of the universe. They simply constitute a normal part of the orderly cause and effects process. These things happen because God doesn't intervene between logical causes and effects. To do so would be to contradict himself since he's the one who created the linkage in the first place. This important theological issue confronts us every time we turn on our TV or open our newspaper. It helps explain famines in Ethiopia, earthquakes in Mexico, and tornadoes in Oklahoma.

Next, we must realize that a dictator God is an anachronism in a democratic world. Believing our God is like a primitive potentate is immoral and undesirable. Trying to maintain a spiritual relationship with such a creator is almost impossible. It nullifies the idea of freedom. It demeans and diminishes men and women, turning them into sycophants. God must represent righteousness (see Deut 32:34). God must exemplify total fairness and impartiality (see Rom 2:11).

Finally, we must accept personal responsibility. God isn't managing affairs in this world; we are! The first divine commandment to the first human beings on earth makes this clear: "God created humans in his image, in the image of God he created them; male and female he created them. God blessed them, and God said to them, 'Be fruitful and multiply and fill the earth and subdue it and have dominion over the fish of the sea and over the birds of the air and over every living thing that moves upon the earth'" (Gen 1:27–28).

Why would God have told us to do these things if he planned to do them himself? Why would he have told us to take control of the world if he planned to retain control himself?

We must be willing to take charge. We are the ones who must care for our environment! We are the ones who will be held accountable for poor management of our air, land, and water. We are the ones who will suffer if we exercise poor stewardship of our natural resources.

We must realize that most unfortunate catastrophes are caused by mankind's own carelessness and selfish behavior. We must understand that for most earthly events, we're the ones who are sovereign! The scripture says, "You have made them a kingdom and priests serving our God, and they will reign on earth" (Rev 5:10).

God created the natural realm, but he expects us to run it! We must grow up and accept responsibility. We are no longer children. We are joint heirs with Christ. If the world is going to get better, it's up to us! Jesus said, "I do not call you servants any longer, because the servant does not know what the master is doing, but I have called you friends, because I have made known to you everything that I have heard from my Father" (John 15:15).

Sometimes, even though we may not express it openly, we probably think, "If I were God, I'd replace pain with pleasure, hostility with love, and ignorance with knowledge. If I were God, I'd make a perfect world."

But how would I do that? Slaves and robots cannot create a perfect world. Only autonomous individuals with initiative and a sense of purpose can make progress and achieve success. So perhaps God is creating a perfect world—only he's not in a hurry. Remember, "with the Lord one day is like a thousand years, and a thousand years are like one day" (2 Peter 3:8). So maybe, as agents of God, we are supposed to be making a more perfect world as we grow and learn and gradually become Christlike.

Paul says, "We work together with [God]" (2 Cor 6:1).

John even envisioned such a perfect world, saying, "The kingdom of the world has become the kingdom of our Lord and of his Messiah" (Rev 11:15). But this won't happen if we expect God to do our job.

The doctrine of divine sovereignty must be reinterpreted because dictators are destructive, human beings have free will, and evil still exists.

Chapter 3

Reinterpreting the Doctrine of the Trinity

The architect conceptualized a marvelous city. He set in motion all the processes necessary to develop it and keep it thriving and growing. When he needed to communicate with the inhabitants at various times, he sent instructions, but the advice often became garbled and distorted in translation. Finally, he sent his own personal emissary to deliver his messages, but some of the people mistook the messenger for the architect. Strangely enough, they insisted that even though the architect was still in his penthouse office at general headquarters, somehow he was also walking their streets. His teachings about love for enemies and disregard for certain rules and regulations angered many people, who finally killed him. After the emissary was no longer physically present, the architect decided to send personal messages to each citizen through their minds and hearts. But the people refused to use their own intellectual abilities and insisted this spiritual guidance system was really a mysterious person. Somehow they believed the architect was still in his office; the emissary he had sent was now sitting at his side; the spiritual guidance system was a third person who had somehow been distributed to multitudes of men and women. Yet they claimed the architect, the emissary, and the guidance system were all one individual.

Arguing about this illogical concept caused much animosity and many destructive conflicts. It distracted the population from productive achievements.

The concept of the Trinity must be reexamined. The description of God as three in one is unnecessarily confusing. It elevates Jesus to be an equal partner with God, and that destroys monotheism. Then it makes the Holy Spirit into a strange mystical creature instead of a wonderful personal aid. Neither of these beliefs is reasonable.

The scripture clearly indicates many distinct intrinsic differences between God the father and God the son. One of the most radical is that God is self-existent. The scripture says, "God began to create the heavens and the earth" (Gen 1:1). Then the psalmist said, "Before the mountains were brought forth or ever you had formed the earth and the world, from everlasting to everlasting you are God" (Ps 90:2).

Jesus said, "The Father has life in himself." Then he explained that his own existence is not from himself but from God, saying, "He has granted the Son to have life in himself.... 'I came from God, and now I am here. I did not come on my own, but he sent me'" (John 5:26; 8:42).

God is omniscient (see 1 John 3:20). Jesus was not omniscient (see Matt 24:36).

God is also omnipotent (see Matt 19:26). Jesus was not omnipotent. He recognized and expressed his personal limitations (see Mark 6:5; John 5:19, 30).

God is omnipresent (see Ps 139:7; Jer 23:24). Jesus was certainly not omnipresent. He could not be in Jerusalem and Bethany simultaneously. Therefore, it's obvious Jesus was not God in an absolute sense.

Many worship phrases extol the belief that God is the greatest of all and his will is supreme: "Yours, O LORD, are the greatness, the power, the glory, the victory, and the majesty, for all that is in the heavens and on the earth is yours; yours is the kingdom, O LORD, and you are exalted as head above all" (1 Chron 29:11). Jesus, on the other hand, is subordinate, and his will is adaptable and submissive: "Yet not what I want but what you want" (Matt 26:39). Over and over, we're told Jesus's power was delegated to him by God (see Heb 3:2).

God is immutable (see Num 23:19). God cannot evolve or develop or change (see Mal 3:6). Jesus, on the other hand, grew and increased in spiritual maturity (see Luke 2:40, 52). We're even told Jesus earned the right to his authority (see Heb 5:8–9).

God can't be contained in earthly vessels (see John 4:24). The scriptures emphasize God's majesty and grandeur (see 1 Kgs 8:27). It is the essence of Jesus, however, that he was flesh and blood and dwelt on this earth (see Luke 24:39). Paul expressly stated that Jesus is not the same as God, saying, "Then the Son himself will also be subjected to the one who put all things in subjection under him, so that God may be all in all" (1 Cor 15:28).

Belief in the Trinity also leads to confusion about the Holy Spirit. This subject of the Holy Spirit is very complicated. It can cause divisiveness and misunderstanding. It can lend itself to superstition and sensationalism. It can lead to unrealistic and destructive behavior.

Most of the problems concerning the Holy Spirit are caused by the fact that early writers did not understand the conscious and subconscious functions of the brain. They did not have the appropriate language tools to interpret psychological principles.

To be helpful, the concept of the Holy Spirit must be something that fits into ordinary, everyday life. It must not be viewed as a supernatural, external creature. Instead, it must be understood and utilized as a natural, internal motivator.

The idea of the Holy Spirit originated to describe God's presence in us. Paul was attempting to explain this when he said, "God's love has been poured into our hearts through the Holy Spirit that has been given to us" (Rom 5:5).

The Holy Spirit enables our conscience to attain access to our highest survival instincts, to take advantage of our best teachings, and to apply our rational skills.

God may be an abstract ideological concept; Jesus may be a concrete historical person; but the Holy Spirit is an internal psychological reality.

Why did the doctrine of the Trinity develop?

Most men and women seem to need a powerful protector. They like to identify with a human helper, and they tend to personalize the Holy Spirit. Therefore, the three persons in one definition of the Trinity continues to be a basic doctrine even though it is problematic and often misunderstood. It was devised to explain the different aspects of spirituality and especially to support the claims of a divine Jesus.

Early theologians believed the virgin birth was necessary for Jesus to be sinless. They thought DNA and inheritance factors came solely through the male line. Women were considered the fertile field, or the incubator, designed to nurture the seed that was deposited by the man.

If this were the case, then Jesus could escape the old Adam taint and the depravity of original sin. Today, however, we know half of all inherited traits are from the woman, who bears an equal responsibility in the genetic process. Therefore, if Mary is human, then Jesus got these human, or depraved, genes through her, and half is enough to taint the whole!

Some religions realized this and tried to solve the problem by making Mary herself to be of immaculate conception—which only succeeded in moving the whole dilemma back one more generation! Jesus would still be contaminated! The doctrine of the Trinity didn't solve that problem.

Then, when the disciples still felt Jesus's presence after his crucifixion, they developed a belief in the Holy Spirit, and this led to the doctrine of the Trinity.

What problems occur as a result of the doctrine of the Trinity?

Belief in the Trinity dilutes the crucial principle of monotheism and humanizes the God of spirit. The deity of Jesus dogma—with a virgin birth, angels, and miracles—causes us to deal with mystical ghosts in a strange other world. This is so unlike the life we live that no parallel to everyday events can be drawn. We can't apply rational explanations or integrate spiritual principles with current scientific knowledge. It makes Christianity so different and unrelated to normal life that it becomes irrelevant.

There is no evidence whatsoever that prophetic scriptures ever expected God to occupy a human body. All of the hopeful, forward-looking expectations envisioned a deliverer and a messenger sent from God. This messiah would embody God's authority and extend God's love. He would reverence God's world and demonstrate God's truth. He would represent God's presence, but no Hebrew prophet ever conceived of a human messiah who would be synonymous or equal with God. That would be idolatrous. The principle of monotheism was too important and hard won to be shaded with such a teaching. Over and over, we hear these words repeated: "Hear, O Israel: The LORD is our God, the LORD alone" (Deut 6:4).

The Hebrews did believe, very strongly, that human beings can be children of the Most High and thus, in one sense, gods (see Ps 82:6). This is the way Jesus should be understood. There are a few verses of Scripture that can be interpreted to mean Jesus is God of very God, but the great preponderance of scriptural evidence points in another direction.

The scripture says, "God cannot be tempted by evil" (Jas 1:13), yet Jesus could be tempted (see Matt 4:1; Heb 2:18).

Jesus had all the normal human emotions. He was frustrated: "I have a baptism with which to be baptized, and what constraint I am under until it is completed!" (Luke 12:50).

Jesus was anxious: "Now my soul is troubled. And what should I say: 'Father, save me from this hour'?" (John 12:27).

Jesus was angry: "He looked around at them with anger" (see Mark 3:5).

Jesus was sad: "When [he] saw her weeping...he was greatly disturbed in spirit and deeply moved.... Jesus began to weep" (John 11:33, 35).

Jesus was surprised: "When Jesus heard him, he was amazed" (Matt 8:10).

Jesus definitely pointed beyond himself in case after case. He said, "Not my will but yours be done" (Luke 22:42); "for I have come down from heaven not to do my own will but the will of him who sent me" (John 6:38). These statements obviously separate the two individuals.

One scripture even says, "Going a little farther, he threw himself on the ground and prayed, 'My Father, if it is possible, let this cup pass from me, yet not what I want but what you want" (Matt 26:39).

Jesus also said, "If I testify about myself, my testimony is not true. There is another who testifies on my behalf, and I know that his testimony to me is true" (John 5:31–32). If Jesus is God of very God, why wouldn't his testimony be valid?

Other scriptures say, "My teaching is not mine but his who sent me.... If I glorify myself, my glory means nothing. It is my Father who glorifies me.... The words that I say to you I do not speak on my own, but the Father who dwells in me does his works.... If you loved me, you would rejoice that I am going to the Father, because the Father is greater than I" (John 7:16; 8:54; 14:10, 28). Again, he separates himself from God!

The writer of Hebrews clearly defines the role and status of Jesus, saying he was the brethren or social equal of the rest of mankind. He was seed of Abraham (see Heb 2:16–17). This indicates Jesus was a normal human being in every respect.

Jesus even disassociated himself from moral perfection, saying, "Why do you call me good? No one is good but God alone'" (Mark 10:18).

He emphasizes his separateness from God by asking, "My God, my God, why have you forsaken me?" (Matt 27:46).

Jesus made a tremendous insightful breakthrough when he dared to say human beings have divine potential. Yes, God was in him, and he was a prototype of what we can be when God is in us!

Jesus prayed for us, saying, "As you, Father, are in me and I am in you, may they also be in us, so that the world may believe that you have sent me. The glory that you have given me I have given them, so that they may be one, as we are one, I in them and you in me" (John 17:21–23).

The scripture says, "For the one who sanctifies and those who are sanctified all have one Father. For this reason Jesus is not ashamed to call them brothers and sisters" (Heb 2:11).

If Jesus is God in disguise, then he provides no valid example for us to follow. A halfway incarnation is no incarnation at all. If he was different from us in quality as well as in quantity, then he's no help as a model. If this is true, then he is not the firstborn among many brethren. It's all a cruel hoax.

Debates about Jesus's humanity, or lack of humanity, are a distraction. They're theoretical and unrelated to daily life.

Reinterpreting the Trinity doesn't devalue Jesus. On the contrary, the momentous life-giving essence of the gospel lies in the fact that Jesus demonstrated what men and women were meant to be. If we can comprehend this earth-shaking doctrine, we'll be able to exhibit both divine confidence and human humility.

Viewing the Trinity in a different and more symbolic way doesn't weaken Christianity. There's no evidence that believing in a Triune God has ever improved personal character or social relationships or increased justice.

How can we reinterpret the doctrine of the Trinity?

First, we must redefine the three terms: God, Jesus, and the Holy Spirit.

The concept of God must not be trivialized or compartmentalized. Jesus said, "God is spirit" (John 4:24). Spirit is not an entity that can be expressed numerically.

God is more than can be expressed. He is infinite! If God could be defined in human words, then he wouldn't be God. An early writer explained, "We can tell what he is not! But we can't tell what he is!" Monotheism is an essential principle. The concept of one creator with the attributes of omniscience, omnipotence, and omnipresence must be maintained.

Next, the humanity of Jesus must be emphasized. The passage that's used to validate the supernatural birth is taken out of context. The Old Testament scripture says, "Therefore the Lord himself will give you a sign…. The young woman is with child and shall bear a son and shall name him Immanuel…. Before the child knows how to refuse the evil and choose the good, the land before whose two kings you are in dread will be deserted" (Isa 7:14–16).

The word translated as *virgin* simply means "a young woman." This was not Mary, because the prophecy continued, saying, "I went to the prophetess, and she conceived and bore a son…. Before the child knows how to call 'My father' or 'My mother,' the wealth of Damascus and the spoil of Samaria will be carried away by the king of Assyria" (Isa 8:3–4). It's obvious all these prophecies were about current political situations, not Jesus's birth.

The specific title "son of God" was not stressed by Jesus, but it has interesting connotations. The Hebrews had few adjectives, so they often used a noun plus the phrase *son of*. Barnabas, "son of consolation," meant he exemplified calmness and comfort. James and John were called "sons of thunder" because they were volatile and excitable. Peacemakers would be called "sons of God" because they reflect the divine spirit of reconciliation. Jesus, "son of God," was Godlike. Such language designated him as an agent of authority, channeling God's purposes through his ministry.

The most miraculous thing about Jesus is that there was nothing miraculous about him! He preferred and constantly used the designation *son of man*, which means "a mortal or human person." That the God of all creation can be manifested in humanity through natural processes is the greatest wonder of all. The people of Jesus's day said, "We know where this man is from, but when the Messiah comes no one will know where he is from" (John 7:27). In other words, because they had seen the ordinary birth and growth and development of this man, they thought he couldn't possibly be the messiah.

The important thing in the Gospels is not that Jesus was God, but rather that God was in Jesus. Paul said, "In Christ God was reconciling the world to himself" (2 Cor 5:19).

This realization has great implications for humanity. If God can be in Jesus and empower Jesus, then he can be in us and empower us! Paul said, "There is one God; there is also one mediator between God and humankind, Christ Jesus, himself human" (1 Tim 2:5).

Finally, the Holy Spirit must not be marginalized.

The only way Jesus's ministry could be continued and his message and mission carried out was for ordinary men and women to be enabled as emissaries. That's what the coming of the Holy Spirit symbolized. Jesus explained this when he said, "As the Father has sent me, so I send you. When he had said this, he breathed on them and said to them, 'Receive the Holy Spirit'" (John 20:21–22).

He was probably referring to Pentecost when he repeated this promise, saying, "You will receive power when the Holy Spirit has come upon you, and you will be my witnesses in Jerusalem, in all Judea and Samaria, and to the ends of the earth" (Acts 1:8).

The Holy Spirit imparts both inspiration and self-confidence. It sharpens our minds to develop new insights, and it enhances our ability to understand spiritual concepts.

God is the Alpha and Omega—all that is great and good. Jesus exemplified humanity at its best. The Holy Spirit is the indwelling spiritual power that enables us to be more than self-absorbed creatures. These three concepts are vitally important; they are positive, productive, and powerful. But it's not logical or helpful to try to combine them into one strange mystical being.

The doctrine of the Trinity must be reinterpreted because monotheism is essential, Jesus is a normal person, and the Holy Spirit is an internal aid that connects us with God.

Chapter 4

Reinterpreting the Doctrine of Vicarious Atonement

The ruler was a paragon of perfection. He tolerated no weaknesses or mistakes, but his subjects were ordinary men and women with normal human frailties. They tried to improve, but they won some and lost some. At times they exhibited love and compassion, but at other times they were selfish and shortsighted. They were gradually learning and growing, but for the ruler this wasn't good enough. He demanded absolute perfection. Nothing less would do. He felt his own holiness and power would somehow be contaminated or compromised if less-than-perfect creatures were allowed into his domain. Because the inhabitants simply couldn't measure up, they were all placed under a death sentence. In fact, it was much worse than mere execution. Instead, an especially cruel and painful torture chamber awaited every man, woman, and youth in the kingdom. Furthermore, there would be no end to this sentence. It would last forever.

Now, the ruler didn't really want all his subjects to suffer forever, yet for some strange reason he insisted upon establishing these rules and enforcing this terrible decree. After many years, when he could think of no other option, he sent his young prince to live among the people for a few years with the understanding that he would eventually be put to death. It seems this senseless scenario would somehow nullify the curse he had imposed on humanity.

In some weird way, the few people who hear about this drama and believe it can make them worthy citizens will then be accepted by the ruler. Unfortunately, however, those who don't hear about it or don't understand and accept it will still be destined for the perpetual torture chamber. We're told this sacrifice will somehow pay the penalty for our sins. But who will it pay? Is it a payment to God to satisfy his wrath or to Satan to ransom our souls? We don't know!

What a preposterous story! Oddly enough, this is a rough description of one of Christianity's basic doctrines.

The vicarious atonement must be reexamined and reinterpreted.

Why would God set up an impossible moral system that requires absolute perfection? There is no provision for trial and error. There is no leeway for learning and development. Everything is black or white. Under this system we're "damned if we do and damned if we don't" because few choices are totally right or totally wrong. Instead, most of life's decisions must be made between the lesser of two evils or the greater of two goods.

If a teacher required students to take a test no one could ever pass, we'd say she was a poor teacher and thus ultimately to blame for the subsequent failures. If parents set unrealistic standards their children could never hope to reach, we'd say they are poor parents and thus ultimately to blame for the inevitable failures. Yet we claim an all-powerful God, who had innumerable options at his disposal, set up an impossible moral system. Since the beginning of time, not one human being has ever succeeded at it. Furthermore, God, who had foreknowledge and knew everyone would fail, still decreed a sentence of eternal torture for not measuring up. The only possible antidote for these sins was the shedding of blood. Something or someone must die!

Why would God do that? Why would he create such a destructive rule? Why would he impose such a terrible consequence?

He wouldn't.

It isn't reasonable to claim that every man and woman on earth is evil enough or has sinned enough to deserve everlasting torture in a place called hell. This doctrine doesn't portray a God who is loving and wise or even humane. Children are certainly not born depraved. Jesus said we should become like them to see the kingdom of heaven (see Matt 18:3).

Of course, nobody is perfect. Everyone has faults and weaknesses that cause problems. But there's a reason for that. We don't come into this world fully equipped. Instead, after birth each individual is expected to grow, mature, and acquire wisdom through a process of trial and error. Therefore, it's obvious that over the years all of us will make mistakes. We'll choose some right actions and some wrong actions. We'll have some successes and some failures. We'll win some and lose some. But that certainly doesn't mean we're such vile, hopeless sinners that we deserve to be punished forever. It simply means this is how we learn and develop as human beings.

Believe it or not, Jesus himself went through this same normal process. The scriptures say, "Although he was a Son, he learned obedience through what he suffered, and having been made perfect, he became the source of eternal salvation for all who obey him" (Heb 5:8–9).

Now, there are definitely evildoers and criminals who must be restrained or eliminated, but most people don't really need constant criticism and censure for their shortcomings. They are already aware of them. They don't even need to be punished for their misdeeds because they are usually sufficiently punished by the consequences of those misdeeds. We reap what we sow. But those penalties that are imposed after death would have no purpose. By then it's too late for discipline or rehabilitation. The pain being inflicted would only be revenge. Furthermore, God can't be all in all if hell continues forever. If suffering and anguish are going to be imposed eternally, then evil has been victorious.

It's significant that when Jesus counseled people, he never asked the question "Do you admit that you're a sinner?" He never shamed, blamed, or threatened anyone—not Zacchaeus, not the woman taken in adultery, not even the thief on the cross. He knew that trying to make people feel unworthy and guilty is psychologically damaging and utterly useless. In fact, he seldom mentioned their sins at all. Instead, he offered forgiveness, encouragement, and hope.

Even Old Testament writers disagreed on these issues of depravity and sacrifice. Early scriptures give elaborate prescriptions for sacrifice (e.g., Exod 20:24). Over the years, a few thoughtful people began to realize that a God of love would never set up a complicated salvation system based on violence and blood sacrifice. Some later scriptures say that no such commandments were ever given. Jeremiah discounted sacrifices (see Jer 7:21–23).

According to the vicarious atonement theory, we're told our depravity is a dreadful human condition caused by Adam's fall. We're all sinful by nature, and our inevitable mistakes merely prove that fact. Since we're born as totally unworthy worms, we deserve a death sentence. Nevertheless, to show his mercy, God decided to provide us with an escape clause. The plan goes like this: "If you believe a certain divine man died to appease my wrath and pay for your sins, then I'll save you, even though you don't deserve it. Unfortunately, if you don't happen to know about this man or get your belief about him exactly right, then you're doomed!"

That isn't good news!

Why would God want to make us feel utterly worthless and evil? Why would he tell us we must forgive unconditionally all those who sin against us yet demand a deadly vicarious payment for all those who sin against him? Well, in fact, he wouldn't!

God didn't set up this complicated salvation system. Even the premise is illogical because according to the rules of this system, Jesus didn't actually "pay the penalty for sin." He would have had to suffer eternal damnation to do that. If mere death is the penalty, then why wouldn't sinners only be annihilated instead of being tortured forever?

A sincere member of an evangelical denomination heard a soul-winning sermon and decided her young son should be converted. She called him in and said, "You're old enough to be accountable. If you were run over by a car and killed, you'd burn in hell." She begged him to kneel and ask God to save him. He did and went back to his ballgame. The mother tearfully reported to her pastor that she had "won her son to the Lord." This describes the common procedure required by this superficial and dangerous theology.

If this particular formula is the only path to heaven, then why didn't Jesus emphasize that fact to the Roman centurion? Instead, after a brief discussion, Jesus complimented his faith (see Matt 8:5–14).

Why didn't he tell the Syro-Phoenician woman about it? Instead, Jesus rewarded her persistence and her clever responses (see Mark 7:25–29).

Why didn't he clarify it to every Samaritan he counseled? Instead, he asked the woman at the well about her background and then simply offered her living water (see John 4:7–20).

Jesus didn't present this salvation formula to anyone. He didn't mention this elaborate substitution system to the sheep in his parable about those being welcomed into the kingdom. These individuals didn't seem to have any religious knowledge or doctrinal beliefs, but he accepted them and rewarded them (see Matt 25:33–46).

When Jesus blessed the little children, he certainly didn't require them to repent and believe in the death, burial, and resurrection. Instead, the scriptures say, "Jesus…said, 'Let the children come to me, and do not stop them, for it is to such as these that the kingdom of God belongs. Truly I tell you, whoever does not receive the kingdom of God as a little child will never enter it'" (Luke 18:16–17).

Why did the doctrine of the vicarious atonement develop?

People have always felt fearful and insecure in a complex world. Theologians conceived of the dreadful doctrine of total depravity because there had to be an explanation for all the evils in our world for the scales of justice to balance.

Also, people need to find reasons for their own less-than-honorable conduct. Most of us realize instinctively that we aren't all we should be. Since we're afraid to admit life may be based on chance, we often attempt to justify tragedy and death.

We can say, "We're good creatures; therefore, good things happen to us." Unfortunately, that's not true in every case. So when bad things happen to us, the only way to balance the scales is to say, "Since bad things happen to us, we must be bad!" Unscrupulous religious leaders have learned you can't force people to behave against their own self-interest unless you can convince them they're depraved and deserving of punishment. This doctrine was useful to ensure absolute obedience in a world of monarchs and selfish religious leaders.

Furthermore, many ancient religions practiced child sacrifice. The Hebrews later mitigated this practice by substituting animal sacrifices. The story of Abraham and Isaac is an illustration of this dreadful custom (see Gen 22:11–13).

Therefore, it's not surprising that Paul would interpret Jesus's death as a way to abolish this practice, saying, "He has rescued us from the power of darkness and transferred us into the kingdom of his beloved Son, in whom we have redemption, the forgiveness of sins" (Col 1:13–14).

What problems occur as a result of the doctrine of the vicarious atonement?

This teaching creates a negative psychological climate. In the first place, a substitute is not a valid guilt alleviator. It doesn't accomplish anything, and it encourages passive surrender, not active responsibility. It allows us to project our weaknesses onto others. Most evangelicals teach that although everyone has the possibility of salvation, only a few individuals accept it. Those who hear the claims of Christ, recognize their lost condition, repent of their sins, and trust Jesus's death, burial, and resurrection for their redemption are saved. Those who don't hear the gospel, or understand it differently, remain lost.

This common view holds that human beings, in their natural state, are creations of God but not children of God. Because they're taught about Adam and Eve's fall and because of their own feelings of guilt, many people believe they must be restored to a divine relationship by personally accepting Christ's atonement on their behalf.

Since there aren't any actual cause-and-effect reasons for the conversion experience and since there are many different beliefs about how to obtain it, this doctrine leads to unnecessary doubts and fears. It separates beliefs from actions. It fragments and weakens our personality. It leads to exclusiveness and pious hypocritical stances. It causes us to condemn those of other faiths. In a diverse world these viewpoints and actions create unnecessary conflict.

Believing in depravity leads to learned helplessness, which prevents growth and lowers self-worth. This doctrine produces divine apple polishers and spiritual bootlickers.

Above all, the vicarious atonement relies on fantasy and magical thinking. There's no reality in the doctrine. It requires compartmentalization because in no other area of life can a substitute act for us, or atone for us, or pay for our mistakes. In all other areas we are personally responsible and accountable.

This teaching builds walls rather than bridges. It excludes all religious groups that don't understand and accept the ancient Jewish sacrificial system. Yet Jesus's gospel tried to bring in rather than shut out. It was inclusive rather than exclusive. He said, "People will come from east and west, from north and south, and take their places at the banquet in the kingdom of God" (Luke 13:29).

Religious intolerance hinders cultural cooperation, harmony, and productivity. More importantly, beliefs that are illogical and primitive cause Christianity to lose credibility in a more educated and mature populace.

Many well-meaning Christians insist upon dividing the population of the world into two distinct categories: the saved and the lost. But this is overly simplistic and, in fact, inaccurate.

In the wonderful parable of the prodigal son, the father indicates that the rebellious boy had always been his child. He says, "This son of mine was dead and is alive again; he was lost and is found!" (Luke 15:24).

Being lost doesn't mean being Satan's child and destined for hell. Being lost doesn't necessarily mean being depraved, evil, or sinful. Instead, it simply means being confused and away from your rightful place in life.

When this prodigal was separated from his father, he was alone, hungry, and miserable. When he was with his father he had love, protection, and every resource he needed. So his circumstances were certainly different, but his relationship with his father was never in doubt.

In the story of the lost coin, that item was a valuable piece of silver all the time. It was never a wooden nickel or a lead slug. While it was lost, however, it was useless. It couldn't fulfill its purpose of providing food or essentials for its owner. But its basic nature never changed.

In the story of the lost sheep, we know it still belonged to the shepherd while it was wandering around in the wilderness. Of course it was more vulnerable to attacks by wild animals, and it had no one to provide food and protection, but its ownership didn't change. The shepherd assures us that this lost animal was definitely his sheep and he was going after it until he found it.

We must realize that categorizing is judging and that's not our responsibility. For instance, when a Muslim man donated a million dollars for a child's lifesaving surgery, how can you convince those parents that this benefactor is lost and will spend his eternity in hell?

Remember, Jesus said, "The bad tree bears bad fruit" (Matt 7:17). So what about people who accomplish so much good for those around them, like Gandhi?

In short, labeling people as saved or lost is destructive. It's almost impossible to respect a person and work comfortably with a person you believe is condemned to hell. This incongruent situation is creating great dissonance in a diverse world.

It's also ludicrous to claim that an intelligent creator, who can formulate the principles of nuclear fission and instigate the process of interplanetary orbits, is concerned with some of the trivial details and irrelevant rules that Christians consider so important. How we sprinkle water on people or put people under the water is surely rather unimportant in the grand scheme of things. What we intone over our wafers and wine is surely not of crucial significance. The proper vocabulary about the Trinity, the Holy Spirit, and the propitiation theory is surely not at the top of God's list of concerns.

Religious indoctrination forces an individual to develop a split personality. As consumers we're urged to get all the facts, analyze the information, and think for ourselves. As citizens we're urged to read and research and consider all sides of the issues. As students we're urged to be skeptical of propaganda and emotional hype. Yet as Christians we're urged to do the opposite. We're told we can't trust our senses. We're told religion isn't necessarily logical. We're told critical thinking borders on rebellion. We're told to just believe, to accept without question, to surrender our mental faculties, and to use faith, not reason. We're told any different views are heresy. We're told if certain doctrines sound irrational or unfair, we're to suppress our doubts because doubts are of the devil.

Why would God set up this dual system? Why would he want us to be helpless and dependent? Why would he want to discourage our intellectual development concerning religious matters? Well, in fact, he wouldn't!

The traditional explanation of the atonement demeans God and misses the entire significance of the incarnation. Supposedly, God, the first person of the Trinity, is angry because of humanity's sin and won't forgive them until a penalty has been paid. So Jesus, the second person of the Trinity, has to die in order to appease divine justice by offering the perfect life and sacrificial death. This suffering somehow satisfies God, so those who believe in this substitution theory are entitled to pardon and salvation. Those who can't believe this artificial transaction is efficacious will burn in hell forever. Shallow, misleading doctrinal interpretations such as this have enervated the gospel.

Evangelicals often describe salvation as something that's achieved through agreeing to a brief formula. But if there is one exact way to move a person from an unsaved position to a saved position, then why didn't Jesus repeat that magical solution to everyone he met? If going through a quick and easy ABC process can change a sinner into a saint, then why didn't Jesus ask each of his followers to complete this process? If a particular "repentance, belief, and commitment" procedure is required before a soul is converted, then why didn't Jesus make that the core of every lesson he taught and every sermon he preached?

When we honestly examine Jesus's witness techniques, we find there is no one formula or process or procedure that will enable a person to achieve salvation. Instead, Jesus seemed to evaluate each individual and express his recommendations in ways to meet that person's explicit needs.

To Jesus, salvation was not simply a ticket to heaven. It was the way to attain an abundant life, for now and for eternity. To James and John he said, "Leave your occupation and follow me." With the woman at the well, he questioned her past problems and said, "Let me quench your thirst with living water." With the rich young ruler, he asked about his moral code and then told him to get rid of his wealth. With one crowd he insisted they should become childlike. With Nicodemus, who obeyed all the rules and considered himself already morally acceptable, because he was of the lineage of Abraham, Jesus advised an entirely new beginning, which he called being born from above. Jesus counseled many people of various faiths and never once demanded they immediately abandon their own religious traditions and subscribe to a different creed.

Salvation means attaining wholeness. Jesus helped each person reach that state, not to satisfy a wrathful God but to ensure that the individual can enjoy a successful and productive life! Believing in a vicarious atonement doesn't help us do that.

How can we reinterpret the doctrine of the vicarious atonement?

First, we must realize the sacrificial element was emphasized because it was part of those people's lives. Paul was truly redeemed and released by believing Jesus was a once-and-for-all sacrifice. This assurance allowed the early disciples to move beyond the old idea that the blood of animals and birds could wash away their sins.

But this explanation was only useful for that time and that place. People who were never taught that guilt can be appeased in this fashion won't be helped by such a belief. It's significant that when Pilate questioned Jesus about his purpose, Jesus's answer did not mention a vicarious atonement. Instead, he said, "For this I came into the world, to testify to the truth" (John 18:37). Jesus lived and died for truth, and Christ arose to show that truth is eternal.

God never established a sacrificial system of propitiation. This strange system was established by human beings. Even several Old Testament writers realized that (see 1 Sam 15:22; Pss 40:6; 51:16–17; Prov 21:3; Hos 6:6; Micah 6:7–8).

The only sacrifice God desires is dedication, morality, and service to others. Paul said, "I appeal to you therefore, brothers and sisters, on the basis of God's mercy, to present your bodies as a living sacrifice, holy and acceptable to God, which is your reasonable act of worship" (Rom

12:1). Jesus said, "Go and learn what this means, 'I desire mercy, not sacrifice'" (Matt 9:13).

Next, we must realize all people are products of their own culture and their own time. Scripture writers couched their insights in king/subject and master/slave language motifs because that was the world they knew. Original thinking and rebellious attitudes presented dangerous threats to the throne and thus were seen as undesirable behavior. Since earthly rulers wanted obedient and submissive subjects, most people concluded God would want the same things.

Ancient theologians couldn't imagine individual autonomy or democratic governments. Their highest concept was that of a benevolent dictator who responded to adoration and rewarded faithful service. Such masters could be influenced by flattery and bribes. Therefore, these less-than-divine traits were often attributed to God. This preoccupation with monarchs who demanded obedience has shaped our theology. But our world today is different, and this autocratic framework is misleading and irrelevant.

Theologians also get hung up on correct liturgies and rituals. That's probably because all of us are creatures of conditioning. Neurotic obsessions are common. When things don't go right, we feel guilty, so we repeat special little procedures to make ourselves feel safer. Our dances and chants and prayers and worship practices are comforting and reassuring. It's easier to recite creeds and perform ceremonies than it is to accept responsibility and make tough decisions. We make up these arbitrary liturgies and act out these mindless rituals for ourselves, not for God.

The doctrine of the vicarious atonement continues because we need relief from guilt and the assurance that God loves us. Today, people need to understand that Jesus did die for us. But he didn't die to satisfy an angry God. He died to ensure truth will prevail. He died to free us from superstition and false teachings.

Finally, we must discover what our God's requirements really are. When someone asked Jesus about this, he gave a short, simple answer, saying, "'You shall love the Lord your God with all your heart and with all your soul and with all your mind.' This is the greatest and first commandment. And a second is like it: 'You shall love your neighbor as yourself.' On these two commandments hang all the Law and the Prophets" (Matt 22:37–39).

Once, Jesus told a story about an injured man who was ignored by several people. Finally, a foreigner stopped. He said, "A Samaritan while traveling came upon him, and when he saw him he was moved with compassion" (Luke 10:33). We call that man the good Samaritan.

Was he good because of who he was? Not at all! In fact, the Samaritans were a despised race of renegades and half-breeds, and Jesus didn't even mention his lineage or his social status.

Was he good because of what he believed? Not at all! In fact, the Samaritans were a heretical, unorthodox religious group, and Jesus didn't even mention his creed or his religious faith.

Was he good because of his high moral code? Not at all! In fact, the Samaritans were considered quite lax in matters of tithing and law keeping, and Jesus didn't even mention his morals or his character.

Why, then, was he called good? Well, he was praised for one thing and one thing only—his concern for his fellow man!

Jesus told another story about two groups who came before the great judge and received unexpected verdicts. The scripture says,

> All the nations will be gathered before him, and he will separate people one from another as a shepherd separates the sheep from the goats, and he will put the sheep at his right hand and the goats at the left. Then the king will say to those at his right hand, "Come, you who are blessed by my Father, inherit the kingdom prepared for you from the foundation of the world, for I was hungry and you gave me food, I was thirsty and you gave me something to drink, I was a stranger and you welcomed me, I was naked and you gave me clothing, I was sick and you took care of me, I was in prison and you visited me." Then the righteous will answer him, "Lord, when was it that we saw you hungry and gave you food or thirsty and gave you something to drink? And when was it that we saw you a stranger and welcomed you or naked and gave you clothing? And when was it that we

saw you sick or in prison and visited you?" And the king will answer them, "Truly I tell you, just as you did it to one of the least of these brothers and sisters of mine, you did it to me." Then he will say to those at his left hand, "You who are accursed, depart from me into the eternal fire prepared for the devil and his angels, for I was hungry and you gave me no food, I was thirsty and you gave me nothing to drink, I was a stranger and you did not welcome me, naked and you did not give me clothing, sick and in prison and you did not visit me." Then they also will answer, "Lord, when was it that we saw you hungry or thirsty or a stranger or naked or sick or in prison and did not take care of you?" Then he will answer them, "Truly I tell you, just as you did not do it to one of the least of these, you did not do it to me." And these will go away into eternal punishment but the righteous into eternal life. (Matt 25:32–46)

Now, why were the ones on the right accepted? Was it because of their correct doctrine? Not at all! Nothing was told of their beliefs. They didn't even know Jesus's name.

Were they praised because they kept all the religious rules? Not at all! Nothing was said about their morality.

Then why were they rewarded? Well, they were accepted, praised, and rewarded for one thing and one thing only—their concern for their fellow men. John said, "Let us not love in word or speech but in deed and truth" (1 John 3:18). This theme of love and concern for others is the real gospel message.

The doctrine of vicarious atonement must be reinterpreted because depravity is unreasonable, sacrifice is a cruel paganistic bribe, and propitiation is an invalid concept.

Chapter 5

Reinterpreting the Doctrine of Supernatural Miracles

The magician had a wonderful wand with which he could perform miracles. He could start and stop the rain. He could heal, and he could kill. He could make rocks fall up and turn straw into gold. Oh, marvel of marvels! His power was limitless.

There were no constraints. He could do absolutely anything! The only catch was that a person had to persuade him to do things on their behalf. If you believed completely in his zapping ability and begged him fervently and regularly, you could sometimes get effects without causes. You could sometimes get rewards without effort.

Of course, many unfortunate people never learned the secret code. These foolish ones actually worked to get results. They thought actions, not magic buttons, were the way to succeed. Of course, those who were able to obtain the magician's favor never turned a finger again. Who would toil and sweat or search and study when you can just push a button? Obviously no one! If there is an easier way, why do it the hard way?

Unfortunately, such magic doesn't produce consistent progress. No one will learn or mature or gain wisdom if they are just waiting and hoping for a lucky break. Supernatural miracles must be reexamined.

Why would God set up an erratic system that puts his spiritual processes and his physical processes in irreconcilable conflict? Many religions emphasize a natural world versus a spiritual world. Furthermore, they teach that physical principles and spiritual principles are contradictory. This causes people to expect events that break natural laws. Why would a God of unity promote such a chaotic system?

If the spiritual and physical realms are at odds, then we can't develop and utilize analogies. We can't learn from parables. Why would God engage in inconsistent, undependable, and unfair practices? Well, in fact, he wouldn't!

If a doctrine is unreasonable, unnatural, and unproductive, then it's not valid. To believe in miracles, you have to constantly rationalize, twist, and justify. You have to make excuses, ignore exceptions, and inflate blessings.

When tragic and illogical things happen, the conflict between trying to believe in a loving God and a powerful God creates a crisis. If a fireman saved two or three children from a burning building and then deliberately let your child die, you'd hate him. If God miraculously healed some children and let your child die, that's the way you'd feel toward him, whether you admit it or not!

Suppose two families pray for protection on the highways, and one group narrowly avoids an accident. They rejoice and thank God for his providential care. However, if the other group isn't so fortunate, then their family must ask, "Why didn't God answer our prayers? Why did he protect those other people and not our loved ones?"

We can't live with this dissonance.

To look at scriptures and beliefs about the legends and references to miracles with new eyes, let's consider these questions: If an angel came into your bedroom and told you that you were pregnant with God's child, wouldn't you remember it? If you gave birth to this child amid spectacular signs, miraculous stars, and heavenly hosts, wouldn't you remember it? All these things and many more supposedly happened to Mary, yet twelve short years later both Mary and Joseph were completely baffled by Jesus's unusual behavior in Jerusalem: "When his parents saw him they were astonished, and his mother said to him, 'Child, why have you treated us like this? Your father and I have been anxiously looking for you.' He said to them, 'Why were you searching for me? Did you not know that I must be in my Father's house?' But they did not understand what he said to them" (Luke 2:48–50).

These parents didn't seem to expect anything extraordinary in his life. If all that's related in the Christmas story really happened to them, then this wasn't a normal human reaction!

If you saw an associate mysteriously turn a tank of water into wine, wouldn't you remember it?

If you saw an associate walk across a lake without the aid of floats or boats, wouldn't you remember it?

If you saw an associate touch two slices of bread and create a thousand loaves out of thin air, wouldn't you remember it?

Jesus's disciples supposedly saw these things and many more, yet they never seemed to expect a supernatural solution to any problem. For instance, once, after supposedly just watching Jesus miraculously feed 5,000 people, the disciples thought Jesus was disturbed because they had forgotten to bring bread (see Mark 8:14–16). If they had just witnessed the feeding incident, why would they worry about buying bread? This wasn't a normal human reaction.

If you saw a friend touch a paraplegic in a wheelchair and give him enough strength to immediately run a race, wouldn't you remember it?

If you saw a friend stop a hearse on the way to a funeral and revive the body inside, wouldn't you remember it?

If you saw a friend go to a cemetery, call out someone's name, watch as the grave opened and a corpse climbed out of its coffin and walked toward you, wouldn't you remember it?

Jesus's disciples supposedly witnessed all these events and many more, yet when danger threatened, none of them seemed to have any expectation that Jesus could revive them if they were killed or even revive himself if death came. Instead, they ran away in the crises and then were in abject grief at his burial, thinking that was the end. Why didn't they wait near the tomb for a few days to find out what happened? If they had seen several dead people brought back to life, this wasn't a normal human reaction.

Once, two children stood looking out the window at an arch of colors in the mist. Suddenly, the older boy made a smug pronouncement: "God makes rainbows! God makes everything!"

"Well," his little brother replied, with a sad glance at their disorganized room, "God sure don't make beds!"

This casual observation expresses a deep theological puzzle. Why does God make rainbows but not beds? Why does God make mountains but not skyscrapers? Why does God make oceans but not bathtubs? What is creation? Where does the divine aspect stop and the human aspect start? What differentiates raw material from finished products? What's the heavenly part, and what's the earthly part?

Understanding this simple question would help us deal with the issue of supernatural miracles and answers to prayer.

As honest observers we must admit that while there is ample evidence that God provides the natural resources, there is no reliable evidence that he ever refines them. For instance, when the Israelites needed food, God set up the natural process that caused manna to form, but he didn't gather or grind or bake it (see Num 11:2, 8). He made iron ore, but he never made a needle!

You see, we can't create worlds and universes and natural resources, but we can make beds; therefore, it's obvious that God's part stops where ours begins!

Why did the doctrine of supernatural miracles develop?

We must remember that Jesus was living among ill-informed people. Many legends could have developed from perfectly normal situations. For instance, telling how Jesus walked on water and calmed the storm might have been his loyal followers trying to prove he was more powerful than all the other spirits and demons that everyone believed controlled the weather and physical elements (see Matt 14:24–32).

The illustration about the coin in the fish's mouth may have been based on the advice Jesus gave Peter about how to earn money for their taxes. Perhaps he told him to "go catch a fish" because that had been his former profession (see Matt 17:27).

People labeled things as supernatural because in primitive times there were no scientific explanations for natural phenomena. Thunder, lightning, hail, floods, volcanos, and earthquakes were viewed as miracles. Today, the belief in miracles persists, in the face of all evidence to the contrary, because we want to experience such wonderful events. We desperately want divine protection in a dangerous world. We seem to need sensational explanations for unexplained phenomenon. Then it's human nature to remember the things that fit with our desires and forget the things that don't.

People often hold on tightly and defend vehemently what they know ain't so because it's easier to deny or cop out on the failures than it is to give up the reassuring theology that "God will take care of me."

Actually, belief in a fairy godmother type of deity has some advantages over the short term. It can reduce worry and stress. It can give some temporary hope and optimism. These positive feelings may make the belief become self-fulfilling to a degree, but there will be long-term damage when it proves to be unreliable.

What problems occur as a result of the doctrine of supernatural miracles?

The trouble begins if things don't work out. When a drought occurs, when the crops are withering, when the animals are dying, when the farmers are hurting, people often call for special prayer meetings. Men and women get together and beg God to send rain.

On the other hand, when a blowout occurs, when a tire goes flat, when a car comes to a halt, when an errand is interrupted, people almost never call for special prayer meetings. Men and women never get together and beg God to produce a new tire.

Now, why not? These are both problems. They both represent legitimate and pressing needs. If God comes to our aid and grants our requests, then why isn't one petition as valid and sensible as the other?

What's the difference between these two situations? Well, droughts are part of complex weather patterns. We don't fully understand all the causes and remedies. We can't resolve the difficulty immediately, and we're definitely not in control.

This problem requires long-term scientific research and foresight and preparation. Human beings are lazy, and it's easier to wait until disaster strikes and then turn to God. Blowouts, on the other hand, are specific, rather simple events. We do understand the causes and remedies. We can resolve the difficulties almost immediately, and we're in control! So we proceed on our own without expecting God to intervene.

Have we forgotten that God told men and women to exercise dominion over the world (see Gen 1:26)? Perhaps we'd better begin developing our knowledge and expertise in all areas because what God expects of us concerning flat tires, he expects of us concerning droughts! Some people use belief in miracles like they do carrying a rabbit's foot, just to be on the safe side. They consider belief in miracles like they do reading and obeying their horoscope because it can't hurt.

But it can hurt! Depending on something false makes you neglect preventive behavior and real protection. It also hurts spiritually and psychologically because when you are disappointed over and over again, you begin to feel cheated, angry, and bitter.

When a group of people flying to a casino to gamble died in a plane crash, a religious fanatic said, "That happened because they were sinners." But why in the world were all the other people on the plane injured and killed? Fortunately, Jesus clearly repudiated that belief. The scripture says, "There were some present who told Jesus about the Galileans whose blood Pilate had mingled with their sacrifices. He asked them, 'Do you think that because these Galileans suffered in this way that they were worse sinners than all other Galileans…? Or those eighteen who were killed when the tower of Siloam fell on them—do you think that they were worse offenders than all the other people living in Jerusalem? No, I tell you'" (Luke 13:1–5).

Once, a group of men were in an accident. Some died, and several were severely injured. But one man proudly proclaimed, "The doctor said I'd never walk again, but God healed me!" That sounds so pious and devout, but it was really a sneaky way of saying, "See how important I am? See what God did for me? I have a special connection with the divine!"

To be honest, few people have ever seen a miraculous event, and even if there were one or two unusual blessings out of a thousand crises, that's too erratic to be helpful. We wouldn't want a parachute that only worked once out of a thousand times or even once out of ten times. If you can't depend on something, it's worse than useless.

The belief in miracles makes its proponents into liars. If they really work, why do we have back-up systems of medicine and science? Why do we have long, hard experimental research projects if prayer alone can solve our problems?

If a doctrine or teaching tends to separate religion from life, then it's not valid. Benjamin Franklin said, "Unless we all hang together, we will all hang separately." Likewise, when your value system pits earth against heaven, the mind against the spirit, and faith against reality, your character is weakened.

Wholeness is essential! Fragmentation is deadly! Making up reasons and looking for excuses and trying to fix things destroys your rational faculties. It forces you to deny facts and lie to yourself. It causes you to build up resentment and hostility. Since you can't admit you're mad at God, you will lash out in other perverse ways.

Miracles would nullify our initiative. If we really could push a prayer button, we wouldn't plan and work. Miracles would cause us to sit on our hands and wait for a bailout. Chickens trained to peck a certain trigger to get corn will sit there and starve, hoping to receive a grain now and then rather than go out and hunt for food! Since most of us don't sit and wait for a miracle, this proves we don't really believe in them! In fact, there's very little difference between the behavior and actions of the skeptics who admit their doubts and the true believers who don't.

Some religions operate on a catch-22 system, only in reverse. They set up no-lose situations that work like this: "If you have faith, God will heal you." Therefore, if you get well, that proves God is a supernatural healer. On the other hand, if you don't get well, that doesn't prove God isn't a supernatural healer. Instead, it merely proves you didn't have the proper faith.

If you only believe, you'll experience a financial bailout. Therefore, if things get better, that proves God is a miracle worker. On the other hand, if things don't get better, that doesn't prove God isn't a miracle worker. Instead, it merely proves you didn't believe enough.

If we'll only "pray" God will divert that predicted hurricane. If the storm misses us, that proves God is a weather manipulator. On the other hand, if it doesn't miss us, that doesn't mean God isn't a weather manipulator. Instead, it merely means "the Lord must have had his reasons."

A prophet says, "God has revealed to me that the world is going to end soon. Let's pray." When the world doesn't end, that never means he was wrong about divine revelation. Instead, it merely means our prayers must have changed God's mind!

This system allows us to make any claims we please and then justify whatever happens. It's a wonderful world when you never have to admit you are wrong!

A belief in miracles can even be deadly. Some groups avoid doctors and surgery and blood transfusions. Others impede scientific research, such as stem cell and organ transplants.

The doctrine of miracles is so inconsistent and undependable that we inevitably develop doubts. These inner conflicts stymie growth. We must have integrity of character. Paul warned us about this when he said, "Have nothing to do with profane and foolish tales" (1 Tim 4:7).

God expects us to use our intellectual abilities: "'Come now, let us argue it out,' says the LORD" (Isa 1:18).

When Jesus said, "You will know them by their fruits" (Matt 7:20), he meant we are to evaluate results and evidence. We should always ask, "What really works?"

A universal belief in miracles would end long-term education and research. If we can do it by spiritual magic, then why do it by slow, laborious methods? There would be no dedication to science if you could depend on miraculous intervention, unrelated to logic or effort.

Miracles don't effect permanent solutions; otherwise, we'd already have a perfect world.

A belief in miracles makes God seem callous and uncaring. Why does he let children die of starvation if he can magically create food? Why do we have famines and floods if God can manage weather so easily? Why does he allow the horrible suffering of babies with birth defects and cancer? No normal person could worship or respect a God who deliberately allows such tragedies if he could fix them.

Some Christians maintain that "God is powerful. He can do anything!" They say those who deny miracles are denying the power of God. That's not so! God's power isn't the question. Integrity is the question! Why would God change from one era to another? Why would God use erratic and unreasonable methods? Why would God operate as a house divided, breaking his own laws?

Denying supernatural miracles doesn't diminish God. Instead, it augments God! It says, "My God is better than that! My God chooses to maintain integrity instead of performing an occasional sensational trick!"

Belief in supernatural miracles is not productive!

How can we reinterpret the doctrine of supernatural miracles?

First, we must realize that if something doesn't work in business, sports, and politics, then it's probably not valid in religion. If a doctrine can't be integrated into all other areas, it's false! What works in one area will work in another. That's the ultimate test. That's the "proof of the pudding."

Assimilation means we can take the precepts and principles of one discipline into all other disciplines. We can't be open-minded in one area and closed-minded in another. We can't be tolerant in one area and intolerant in another. We can't be realistic in one area and delusional in another. The human psyche simply cannot function with such dissonance.

Christians in the twenty-first century are struggling to resolve this incongruity. They have one foot on practical truth and one foot on sentimental tradition. That won't work!

Next, we must examine Jesus's methods of healing. It's significant that they were not of the finger-snapping variety. He must have used ordinary powers that are available to us because he said, "Very truly, I tell you, the one who believes in me will also do the works that I do and, in fact, will do greater works than these, because I am going to the Father" (John 14:12).

It's true that we do even greater things. Thousands of blind people are healed every day. Many who suffer are given new life through organ transplants. But these are the results of scientific discoveries, technological inventions, and modern research in areas of medicine and surgery.

Today, if an evangelist claims to raise the dead, we laugh. When a family kept a loved one's body in a freezer, believing she'd be resurrected on the third day, we labeled them insane.

If healing can be accomplished by a touch or a few drops of saliva or a bit of clay, why do we have antibiotics and rehabilitation hospitals?

Finally, we must understand and utilize the power of faith. Faith isn't a preacher yelling "Heal!" It's Columbus sailing on and on to find land! It's Madam Curie doing her thousandth radium experiment! It's Edison trying day after day through innumerable failures to perfect a light bulb.

Believing there are meaningful answers is faith! Accepting the responsibility of learning and working to improve life is faith!

The opposite of faith is not doubt. The opposite of faith is apathy and inertia. Without faith, life becomes the ultimate exercise in futility. A philosopher expressed it this way, saying, "The absence of faith is like a blind man in a dark room looking for a black hat that's not there."

We now know that the mind is a great disease healer. Paralysis, ulcers, skin problems, and innumerable physical conditions can be alleviated through mental and emotional adjustment. In fact, the placebo effect can be powerful.

Both God and Jesus viewed creation as good (see Gen 1:31). Since God doesn't rescind his original plans, all natural processes must be good and consistent with creation. We know Jesus's acts did not clash with natural laws. They only seemed to clash with the laws that were known at the time. Remember, as late as 1900, many reputable physicists vehemently denied the existence of atoms!

In Jesus's day, many events were called miracles because no one understood scientific principles. If we had told a nineteenth-century audience that technologists would soon send pictures through the air, they'd have said, "Only if they can work a miracle." But now we do that every day and call it TV and internet.

If we took a native of the tropics who didn't understand climate changes to Alaska in summer and told him that in a few months he would be able to walk across a certain lake, he would say, "Only if we can work a miracle."

It's astonishing to realize God's gift of electricity could have been enjoyed in the dark ages if scientists had only discovered its possibilities earlier. It's obvious we are in charge of our progress. The belief that we can pray for divine intervention, if worse comes to worse, is false.

The doctrine of supernatural miracles must be reinterpreted because it breaks natural laws, it's inconsistent, and it undermines personal human initiative.

Chapter 6

Reinterpreting the Doctrine of a Literal Hell

The inventor had a crystal ball that helped him see into the future. Even as he made his unique beings, he was aware of their final fate. As a foreseer of events, he knew full well that most of his wonderful creations would end up in the horrendous furnace below his shop. In fact, he had purposely set up this strange system of operation. Every puppet was carefully designed and then set free to learn and grow, but there was a catch. One small slip-up or mistake consigned the unfortunate creature to unbelievable torture. The inventor knew that not a single being could possibly live up to his strict regulations. Yet, as ridiculous as it may seem, he still continued this horrible charade.

He didn't just destroy the defective puppets when they failed to live up to his standards. Instead, for some totally unfathomable reason he decreed that they must endure pain forever in a neither life nor death state of limbo.

Now, to be fair, we must admit that he did provide a loophole. He devised a complicated process whereby these puppets could escape their awful fate. He decided he would let one innocent man die for all the creatures. Somehow, this senseless act was supposed to eradicate everybody's sin and atone for their mistakes. Those who accepted this sacrifice on their behalf could escape perdition, but the majority of the individuals never knew about this plan. Many others misunderstood it or failed to get the formula right.

The doctrine of a literal hell must be reexamined.

Three words in the Bible have been translated into English as *hell.* Sheol, Hades, and Gehenna. *Sheol* is used in the Old Testament to mean, simply, "a place of the dead." *Hades* is used in the New Testament; it is a general term, meaning "the abode of those departed from the earth or in the grave." Jesus used the term *Gehenna,* which was actually a geographical location near Jerusalem. The Valley of Hennon was once considered demonic. The bodies of criminals were thrown there, and garbage is burned there. Gehenna symbolizes a desolate, miserable place of alienation, waste, and destruction.

Fire is a common biblical theme because it served several purposes. Fires can test and evaluate (see 1 Cor 3:13; 1 Peter 1:7).

Fires also purify (see Isa 1:25; 6:6–7; Mal 3:3).

Fire is even connected to the Holy Spirit. John the Baptist said, "I baptize you with water for repentance, but the one who is coming after me is more powerful than I, and I am not worthy to carry his sandals. He will baptize you with the Holy Spirit and fire" (Matt 3:11).

Scripture attempts to describe this remarkable experience, which would occur on the day of Pentecost, saying, "Divided tongues, as of fire, appeared among them, and a tongue rested on each of them. All of them were filled with the Holy Spirit and began to speak in other languages, as the Spirit gave them ability" (Acts 2:3–4).

The same fire that consumes straw transforms clay pots into useful vessels. So, you see, fire is used in many ways, but the one that most Christians are concerned with is the fires of hell.

No subject causes more pain, anxiety, neurosis, and misery than this subject of hell. Unfortunately, people don't realize that most of the devils with pitchforks and demons with tails that populate our nightmares are based on Dante and other writers of medieval literature rather than scriptures.

In fact, there are many serious problems with the traditional doctrine of hell. For example, several of Jesus's own remarks concerning hellfire were directed at his disciples! These were believers, not lost sinners. The scriptures tell us that when his disciples came to him, he began to teach them and said, "If you are angry with a brother or sister, you will be liable to judgment, and if you insult a brother or sister, you will be liable to the council, and if you say, 'You fool,' you will be liable to the hell of fire.... If your right eye causes you to sin, tear it out and throw it away; it is better for you to lose one of your members than for your whole body to be thrown into hell. And if your right hand causes you to sin, cut it off and throw it away; it is better for you to lose one of your members than for your whole body to go into hell" (Matt 5:22, 29–30).

Now, Jesus knew that if anyone would be going to heaven, it would be these men who faithfully followed him. He even promises, "I will come again and will take you to myself, so that where I am, there you may be also" (John 14:3).

If these disciples were saved and secure as far as eternity is concerned, then what did Jesus mean with these warnings about hell?

The scriptures themselves are ambiguous as to their definitions of hell. Some deny its existence (see Eccl 3:19–20). Some use hell to mean trouble (see Ps 116:3). It's also used symbolically (see Rev 20:14).

Jesus used the word *hades* to mean total destruction of a city when he said, "And you, Capernaum...will be brought down to Hades. For if the deeds of power done in you had been done in Sodom, it would have remained until this day" (Matt 11:23).

These scriptures indicate that hell is not necessarily a geographical place. The concept of hell is more concerned with a state of being than with a location. In fact, since Jesus said the kingdom of heaven can be within us, perhaps hell can also be within us.

Several scriptures indicate there will be complete annihilation of that which is evil and nonproductive. Jesus said, "Fear the one who can destroy both soul and body in hell" (Matt 10:28).

The word *destroy* means just that! It insinuates total disintegration! It suggests a blotting out, a vanishing, not a state of perpetual torture.

Why did the doctrine of a literal hell develop?

Teachings about depravity are used to explain evil and justify condemnation. But the idea of eternal perdition is reprehensible in a humane world. Why would God set up a horrible, non-redemptive punishment system that emphasizes pain and torture? Is this utter waste necessary? Can nothing be reclaimed or salvaged? Worse yet, we're told God has prepared such cruel consequences that unregenerated people aren't just annihilated; instead, they are subjected to excruciating agony forever. Since no discipline or rehabilitation is possible at that point, these horrors represent vengeance at its worst. No madman or criminal or monster in the history of the world has ever imposed this kind of suffering. Today, hell would be labeled as cruel and unusual punishment, and that's outlawed in all civilized nations.

Why would God do that? Why would he choose such senseless methods? Why would he advocate completely negative and irredeemable penalties? Why would he inflict a kind of torture that's repudiated by most countries today? Well, in fact, he wouldn't!

God didn't set up this non-redemptive punishment system. It's human beings who formulated and perpetuated these themes of hellish misery and anguish. They did it because many of them were hurt, frightened, and angry. This made them want to lash out in retaliation. They wanted their enemies to suffer. Since they felt that way, they assumed God did too, and he was powerful enough to do what he pleased: "Vengeance is mine…says the Lord" (Rom 12:19).

Historically, men and women have attributed to God their own worst instincts. But as civilization progresses and moral sensitivity increases, these doctrines begin to look barbaric.

What problems occur as a result of the doctrine of a literal hell?

If a doctrine or teaching promotes questionable behavior or sets immoral standards of conduct, then it's invalid. In an age of human rights and civil liberties, we know even flawed human beings are better than that. No civilized country on the face of the earth today publicly condones torture. Therefore, a belief in an everlasting burning hell begins to be an embarrassment to a religion of love.

Hell does not achieve justice! You can't achieve justice by replacing one evil with a worse evil.

Justice must rectify, mitigate, or prevent evil. The doctrine of hell doesn't do that. Believing in hell makes us callous and cruel. It legitimizes violence and revenge. After all, if God does it, why shouldn't we?

Emphasizing hell and demons also encourages superstition! It gives credence to possessions and exorcisms. Then, when kids are fascinated by demonology and psychotic criminals commit atrocities in Satan's name, we're horrified.

It also gives evil an eternal quality. Instead of annihilation, it will live on and on, imposing its suffering forever. That's not victory!

Many people are obsessed with the idea of a personal devil. In fact, many people are obsessed with strange creatures in general. From little green men on Mars to red-suited Lucifers in hell, we like to picture our concepts. Movies, novels, and even scriptures tend to personify good and evil. So is there a personal devil? Well, of course our sins and weaknesses are personal, but the notion of one particular demonic being is counterproductive. Jesus used the term *Satan* in a symbolic way. Once, when Peter rebuked him, Jesus said, "Get behind me, Satan! For you are setting your mind not on divine things but on human things" (Mark 8:33). The sin was in Peter's own mind. Jesus didn't mean Peter had suddenly turned into a supernatural creature; instead, he simply meant Peter's advice was wrong and destructive.

The term *Satan* was also used concerning Judas. The scripture says, "After he received the piece of bread, Satan entered into him" (John 13:27). Again, John obviously didn't mean a supernatural creature had crawled inside Judas's body. Instead, he simply meant Judas had made a deadly decision.

Sometimes our overly dramatic representations strengthen the very thing we're trying to eliminate. Regarding Satan as a powerful supernatural creature gives flesh to a ghost and substance to an illusion. It makes evil infinitely more interesting! It attracts and encourages immaturity. It triggers destructive behavior in psychotic individuals.

It also helps us duck our responsibility. If the devil made me do it, then I'm not to blame. It's easy to create immoral scapegoats and call them Satan. Unfortunately, however, evil is not a neat entity that can be embodied in a creature with horns, a tail, and a pitchfork. Evil is mixed with all we are and all we do. Evil is in us. Whatever hinders our growth, weakens our faith, or tempts us to sin is our personal devil. Any strange creatures or demonic beings are figments of our sick imagination.

Our ideas concerning God's judgment and hell even affect our legal system in the twenty-first century. Judicial codes are based on the doctrine of retribution and punishment. The "eye for an eye" concept is still operative. This leads to irrational conflicts. In our courts we have sticky problems of guilty or not guilty, sanity or insanity, manslaughter or murder. If we could simply abolish the revenge element, we could approach these problems much more sensibly. When a crime is committed, what would be the best solution for both this victim and society as a whole? Mitigating past harm and preventing future harm should be the goals of justice. But victims, as well as the population as a whole, usually want revenge. They don't want to use drugs or therapy to change the perpetrator. They want a penalty involved that will make him suffer for his crime. This does absolutely no good. It doesn't undo the deed or repair the damage. It merely inflicts more evil and sets up a relentless chain of ever-increasing violence.

The doctrine of eternal perdition with its emphasis on hell, judgment, and degrees of suffering makes evil everlasting and fosters fear and revenge. It uses threats and twists emotions. It causes mental illness and engenders hostile feelings. It validates vindictiveness and retaliation. It's out of step with progressive humane attitudes. And it's certainly out of step with a God of love.

There is no perfection as long as evil exists anywhere! There is no victory involved in a process that imposes a permanent, non-rehabilitative, eternal punishment!

How can we reinterpret the doctrine of a literal hell?

First, we must get beyond the animalistic desire for retaliation. We must realize that when the scriptures refer to eternal punishment, they really mean evil is constantly and ultimately being annihilated and good is constantly and ultimately being rewarded. The details of these principles are to be understood symbolically.

In fact, there are several descriptions of this punishment. The scriptures sometime describe hell as alienation. This is the greatest evil that can befall an individual. After Cain killed his brother Abel, he was banished and forced to be a vagrant and a wanderer: "Cain said to the LORD, 'My punishment is greater than I can bear! Today you have driven me away from the soil, and I shall be hidden from your face" (Gen 4:13–14).

Among primitive people, the words *enemy* and *stranger* were synonymous. They assumed, "If he's not of us, he's against us." Therefore, anyone "beyond the circle of the tribal fire" was an alien. It was a fearful thing to be outside this realm of safety. Thus, being thrust into outer darkness was a terrible penalty for arrogance and selfishness. Jesus said, "Many will come from east and west and will take their places at the banquet with Abraham and Isaac and Jacob in the kingdom of heaven, while the heirs of the kingdom will be thrown into the outer darkness" (Matt 8:11–12).

He explained that the chasm of separation is wide and permanent, saying, "Between you and us a great chasm has been fixed, so that those who might want to pass from here to you cannot do so, and no one can cross from there to us" (Luke 16:26).

The truth about hell is not burning bodies; rather, it's a warning of alienation from God and loved ones and all that is good!

Next, the scriptures describe hell as deprivation. None of us likes to lose things. Fires, floods, and bankruptcies are devastating because of the losses involved. Jesus says irresponsible people will have their talents and resources taken away. When he told the parable about the man who refused to invest his talent, he was angry, saying, "Take the talent from him, and give it to the one with the ten talents. For to all those who have, more will be given, and they will have an abundance, but from those who have nothing, even what they have will be taken away" (Matt 25:28–29).

Another great deprivation is loss of liberty. Several times the idea of bondage is suggested. One of Jesus's parables describes an arrest scene: "Bind him hand and foot, and throw him into the outer darkness" (Matt 22:13).

Peter mentions chains: "[God] committed them to chains of deepest darkness to be kept until the judgment" (2 Peter 2:4).

Jude also mentions chains: "The angels who did not keep their own position but deserted their proper dwelling, he has kept in eternal chains in deepest darkness for the judgment" (Jude 6).

Hell depicts the misery of being deprived of all the pleasures and necessities of life.

Finally, the scriptures describe hell as destruction. God hates waste. Jesus talks much of productivity and fruit-bearing. He even had his disciples gather up the fragments of the fish and loaves when he fed the multitude. Nature wastes nothing! The ultimate evil of the universe, therefore, is utter waste! That's the picture of Gehenna. It's a trash heap of garbage and worthless things!

Fires don't punish; they annihilate. Jesus said the tares of evil will be burned up: "Collect the weeds first and bind them in bundles to be burned" (Matt 13:30).

Chaff burns up. Jesus said, "The chaff he will burn with unquenchable fire" (Matt 3:12). Indeed, all that is offensive burns up: "The Son of Man will send his angels, and they will collect out of his kingdom all causes of sin and all evildoers, and they will throw them into the furnace of fire" (Matt 13:41–42).

Several scriptures indicate a complete annihilation of that which is evil and nonproductive. John calls it "the second death," or the absolute end (see Rev 2:11). This concept is used to denote the final, overall destruction of evil. Burning the garbage gets rid of the bacteria, the decay, and the disease.

Now, it's obvious that none of these models is to be taken literally, because the light of the fire and the gloom of the darkness are not even compatible descriptive terms. Jesus said, "So it will be at the end of the age. The angels will come out and separate the evil from the righteous and throw them into the furnace of fire, where there will be weeping and gnashing of teeth" (Matt 13:49–50).

In other verses, torture and hell are described as something that will occur in the presence of Christ and the angels: "[Those who worship the beast] will be tormented with fire and sulfur in the presence of the holy angels and in the presence of the Lamb" (Rev 14:10). Now, surely this horrible event will not take place in heaven. It's obvious these are merely symbolic representations intended to indicate the final and absolute annihilation of evil.

We simply don't know enough to be dogmatic about the details. Those who dispute and argue over such things are wasting their time and energy. Paul foresees a time when truth and righteousness shall prevail and no evil shall remain, saying, "When all things are subjected to him, then the Son himself will also be subjected to the one who put all things in subjection under him, so that God may be all in all" (1 Cor 15:28).

A loving God cannot be all in all as long as unremitting pain is occurring. The scriptures envision a time of perfection, when evil will be ultimately defeated and abolished. John describes the future this way: "I saw a new heaven and a new earth, for the first heaven and the first earth had passed away, and the sea was no more.... [God] will wipe every tear from their eyes. Death will be no more, for the first things have passed away.... Nothing accursed will be found there any more" (see Rev 21:1, 4; 22:3). This indicates there will be a final time and state that is free of tears, pain, and death. Therefore, we know men and women are not being tortured forever in hell!

The doctrine of a literal hell must be reinterpreted because it advocates revenge, it serves no redemptive purpose, and it prevents evil from ever being totally abolished.

Chapter 7

Reinterpreting the Doctrine of a Physical Second Coming

Once, a master engineer planned a grand municipality. He set it up with every institution and resource necessary for a good life. He nurtured a community of families and provided training in every skill. As they made mistakes and achieved victories, they learned by trial and error. But as they made progress, the engineer was holding a time bomb that had already been set to blow the entire project to smithereens.

He told a few confidants the catastrophe was coming. He even warned of signs to denote its approach. But he also said, "It doesn't really matter what you do. It's all pre-planned. The explosion is inevitable. I'll take a few of you out before this happens, but the results of your labor, and any improvements and achievements you make in the meantime, won't matter in the least. Your only mission is to be prepared for this day of destruction." Under these circumstances there would be no motivation for anyone to conserve resources, provide upkeep, or encourage growth.

The idea of a physical second coming with a rapture and a disastrous end time must be reexamined.

The words used in connection with this event are enlightening. It's significant that the ordinary word for "coming" as a physical act is not always the one chosen. Instead, the scripture often includes terms that can mean "to be present or to be near."

Once, it uses a term that means "disclosure or revelation" (see 2 Thess 1:7).

Then it uses a term that means "appearing and brightness" (see Titus 2:13).

It also uses a term that means "to make an appearance" (see Rev 22:7).

Old Testament prophets had made many promises concerning the coming of the messiah (see Isa 9:7; Amos 9:11).

The psalmist foretold, "May he have dominion from sea to sea and from the River to the ends of the earth. May his foes bow down before him, and his enemies lick the dust.... May all kings fall down before him, all nations give him service" (Ps 72:8–9, 11).

Scholars also picked up some old statements from Daniel to support this view: "I saw one like a human being coming with the clouds of heaven.... To him was given dominion and glory and kingship, that all peoples, nations, and languages should serve him" (Dan 7:13–14).

Now, the Christ does come—a first, a second, a third, and a thousandth time—but not as the main character in a science-fiction scenario. He comes every time the Holy Spirit works within a Christian's heart and soul and life to give insight and guidance.

Why did this doctrine of a physical second coming develop?

As usual, most people interpreted these prophetic promises literally. Then, when these events didn't happen at Jesus's first coming, they felt they had to postpone them and anticipate a physical second coming.

Furthermore, many people are preoccupied with the second coming and premillennial details because these subjects are sensational and exciting. They provide eager individuals with a religious version of astrology and science fiction. But they are also very confusing and destructive.

It's important to remember that figures of speech are common in the scriptures. We read phrases such as "My sheep hear my voice," "I am the door," "Abraham's bosom," "The bride of Christ," "Take my yoke," and "Eat my flesh, and drink my blood." But none of these is ever taken literally. Indeed, consider what outlandish doctrines could be concocted if, centuries from now, some of our idioms were misunderstood and taken out of context. Common phrases have little meaning unless you know how and why they originated.

Of course, these phrases are not meant to be taken literally. The writers of Scripture used analogies just as scientists today use models to help explain complex ideas to nonprofessional people. Those models of atoms and DNA chains pictured in textbooks are not factual, but they do express truth.

Biblical language is especially symbolic because individuals in that culture tended to think that way and also because what the writers were attempting to express was almost beyond human ability to comprehend. We may not understand all these things, even today, but that doesn't mean we shouldn't continue to question, explore, and utilize every available tool at our disposal. We must do theological, biological, technological, and scientific research.

Hosea said, "My people are destroyed for lack of knowledge!" (4:6). That's so true! All of us need to have access to as much information as we can understand. For instance, if a two-year-old has to have an operation, his parents can't fully explain all the reasons and necessities of his condition. He has to trust his parents and believe that whatever happens is for his good, even if it seems painful at the time. As soon as he can understand, however, he has a right to know, and the purpose and processes should be explained as fully as possible. It's important for him to realize his parents are not deliberately trying to keep him ignorant. The reason they don't explain everything is only because his immature mind cannot grasp the total significance of the situation. This illustrates how God's revelation deals with our imperfect faith in difficult times.

What problems occur as a result of the doctrine of a physical second coming?

Arguing about this subject wastes time and encourages sensationalism. Even if such an actual literal event is going to take place, it is still not a productive subject of study for most people. Over the years countless theologians have wrangled, authors have written, preachers have preached, and laymen have disputed about these speculations. For those millions of individuals, there was no second coming! If these people had spent that much energy on the great life-and-death issues, it would have been much more beneficial. Thousands have fought over these insolvable puzzles and ignored the basic social problems that could have been alleviated.

Suppose a man left his farm in charge of workers with orders as to what he wanted done about the crops and harvests. Suppose he warned, "Now, someday I'll return to evaluate your progress, so be expecting me!" Would he want them to stand at the gate every day with binoculars looking down the road for his appearance? Of course not! Would he want them to sit and meditate over a possible date for his return? Of course not! Would he want them to meet in discussion groups every day, debating about whether he would come on a horse, in a carriage, or on foot? Of course not! This farm manager would expect them to go to work, accept responsibility, and remember they will be held accountable. Jesus doesn't want us to spend our time trying to discover the details of his possible return; rather, we should focus on learning and applying his principles of ministry.

If someone suggests the return of Christ may be spiritual rather than literal, however, many will protest. They are the same ones who would have insisted Jesus's first coming didn't fulfill prophecy. When Jesus was on earth, many things that had been foretold emerged in different forms than had been expected. An Old Testament scripture says, "I will send you the prophet Elijah before the great and terrible day of the LORD comes" (Mal 4:5). Now, that didn't happen in a literal sense! But Jesus interpreted it symbolically, saying, "If you are willing to accept it, [John] is Elijah who is to come" (Matt 11:14).

Besides all the rational and psychological problems with a physical second coming, there are insurmountable scriptural ones. Those who believe and propagate this doctrine so fervently gloss over numerous conflicting and inconsistent statements. Jesus said, "So when you see the desolating sacrilege, spoken of by the prophet Daniel, standing in the holy place (let the reader understand), then those in Judea must flee to the mountains; the one on the housetop must not go down to take things from the house; the one in the field must not turn back to get a coat. Woe to those who are pregnant and to those who are nursing infants in those days! Pray that your flight may not be in winter or on a Sabbath" (Matt 24:15–20).

Now, this is surely not the rapture. If so, advice about "fleeing to the mountains, praying about pregnancy, and worrying about being cold in winter" is ridiculous.

Another scripture says, "When you hear of wars and rumors of wars, do not be alarmed; this must take place, but the end is still to come. For nation will rise against nation and kingdom against kingdom; there will be earthquakes in various places; there will be famines. This is but the beginning of the birth pangs.... Beware, for they will hand you over to councils, and you will be beaten in synagogues" (Mark 13:7–9). Of course, all these things have happened numerous times over the centuries, and no second coming has occurred.

Another scripture says, "If anyone says to you at that time, 'Look! Here is the Messiah!' or 'Look! There he is!'—do not believe it. False messiahs and false prophets will appear and produce signs and wonders, to lead astray, if possible, the elect. But be alert; I have already told you everything. But in those days, after that suffering, the sun will be darkened, and the moon will not give its light, and the stars will be falling from heaven, and the powers in the heavens will be shaken. Then they will see 'the Son of Man coming in clouds' with great power and glory. Then he will send out the angels and gather the elect from the four winds, from the ends of the earth to the ends of heaven" (Mark 13:21–27).

Most of these things have not happened. But Jesus certainly seemed to expect them to take place within thirty or forty years. It's obvious he was speaking about something imminent because he said, "When they persecute you in this town, flee to the next, for truly I tell you, you will not have finished going through all the towns of Israel before the Son of Man comes" (Matt 10:23).

He also said, "Truly I tell you, there are some standing here who will not taste death before they see the Son of Man coming in his kingdom.... Truly I tell you, this generation will not pass away until all these things have taken place" (Matt 16:29; 24:34).

Zealous premillennialists never explain these passages.

The eschatological doctrines are destructive because they discourage productive action. Why should we work for a lifetime to find a cure for cancer or an alternative energy source or a political solution for world conflicts if we're expecting a supernatural bailout or a cataclysmic disaster at any moment? Some dedicated young people feel they should be out soul-winning instead of going to college if the end is so near. Some politicians vote against clean air and pollution control because they think the end is near!

This belief also undermines humanity's autonomy and robs us of the pleasure and satisfaction of accomplishment. If I've carefully planned and diligently worked on a project and at the last minute someone snatches it away and either zaps it into oblivion or magically brings it to completion, I'd feel cheated.

A physical return of Jesus validates the old fairytale view of life in which the rescuer, the knight in shining armor, the prince on the white horse, or the fairy godmother always swoops down at the last moment and resolves all conflict. This smacks of wishful thinking and immaturity.

Most eschatological beliefs are incongruent with nature, history, and reason. No other event has ever come out of the blue, unrelated to physical laws and human endeavor. Even Jesus's birth was totally unrecognized by those who had the idea of a supernatural messiah arriving in the clouds, disconnected from earthly processes. Instead, he was born, lived, taught, and served in ordinary ways. He wouldn't even fulfill scripture by jumping off the temple (see Matt 4:6–7). He consistently refused to use spectacular or unusual powers. This should tell us something about God's methods.

A belief in a physical second coming stymies progress. You wouldn't spend money and energy remodeling a house if you knew it was going to be demolished shortly. That's why the expectation of a rapture nullifies all incentive to improve cultural conditions. It discourages our motivation to act. Long-term progress becomes unimportant, and that's potentially fatal to any civilization.

Why pray and work for "thy kingdom to come on earth as it is in heaven" if the plan is already made and the hour is already set for the supernatural descent of a mystical kingdom? A divinely imposed kingdom discounts humanity's autonomy and efforts. It keeps us from relying on our own resources and developing our own potential. What good are painfully acquired skills and hard-won knowledge in such a system? Our technological abilities and ethical values would be useless. The time and natural resources that have been invested over thousands of years in the gradual improvement of mind, body, and spirit would have been entirely wasted.

Over the centuries, dozens of physical second comings have been predicted, and none of them have materialized. This destroys our credibility. How many times can we "cry wolf" and still be heeded? From Paul's time until now, the easiest way to create interest and draw crowds has been to proclaim sensational prophecies. Such exciting, pseudo-spiritual themes appeal to the worst in people. They cause fear and anxiety. They increase selfish desires as we anticipate a paradise for me and an inferno for my enemies.

When this marvelous event doesn't happen generation after generation, evangelists give God an excuse by saying, "He is long-suffering and patient." He's postponing judgment because he's "not wanting any to perish" (2 Peter 3:9). But if that's the case, he's deluded, since every day more and more people are being born, only to be lost!

If a doctrine or teaching tends to increase despair or undermine hope, then it's not valid. A doctrine must encourage interest in this world. It must relate to everyday occurrences and common sense. It must be supported by life experiences.

The emphasis of a physical second coming encourages pessimism and negativity. We see what we expect, and this view causes us to expect a worse and worse world. Some fanatical prophets even seem to be glad when evil flourishes because that proves the end time is approaching.

This doctrine encourages irresponsibility and discourages long-term research, preparation, and growth. It divorces life from religion. It elevates trivial sensationalism. It ignores historical precedence as it deals with beasts and marks.

If a doctrine or teaching hinders the growth of knowledge and productivity, then it is not valid!

How can we reinterpret the doctrine of a physical second coming?

First, we must redefine the meaning of *coming*. Jesus indicated that sometimes the word he used can refer to the manifestation of the Holy Spirit at Pentecost. He said, "I tell you the truth: it is to your advantage that I go away, for if I do not go away, the Advocate will not come to you, but if I go, I will send him to you. And when he comes, he will prove the world wrong about sin and righteousness and judgment" (John 16:7–8).

Peter, likewise, confirmed that many of the prophecies about the future were being fulfilled. He addressed the crowd, saying, "Fellow Jews and all who live in Jerusalem, let this be known to you, and listen to what I say…. This is what was spoken through the prophet Joel: 'In the last days it will be, God declares, that I will pour out my Spirit upon all flesh, and your sons and your daughters shall prophesy, and your young men shall see visions, and your old men shall dream dreams. Even upon my slaves, both men and women, in those days I will pour out my Spirit, and they shall prophesy. And I will show portents in the heaven above and signs on the earth below, blood, and fire, and smoky mist. The sun shall be turned to darkness and the moon to blood, before the coming of the Lord's great and glorious day.'… This Jesus God raised up, and of that all of us are witnesses. Being therefore exalted at the right hand of God and having received from the Father the promise of the Holy Spirit, he has poured out this that you see and hear" (Acts 2:14, 16–20, 32–33).

An emphasis on strange signs and wonders is distracting and detrimental to progress. Valid theology must provide basic guidelines for all people, and a belief in an imminent physical second coming opposes innovation in technology, science, and philosophy. Intellectuals are being excluded from Christianity because they can't sincerely hold these beliefs about an imminent physical second coming and still be willing to invest their lives in academic and scientific endeavors.

Next, we must realize and admit that an expectation of Jesus's impending physical return was probably useful in the first century of the Christian era, when believers were in positions of subservience and enduring persecution. When people were helpless slaves, suffering martyrdom, then this doctrine may have given aid. It may have sustained them and provided the hope that was necessary for life. But once people become autonomous, free, and self-determining, as in a democracy, it is definitely a detriment.

Instead of obsessing about prophecies and beasts and anti-Christs, we should follow Paul's advice: "Whatever is true, whatever is honorable, whatever is just, whatever is pure, whatever is pleasing, whatever is commendable, if there is any excellence and if there is anything worthy of praise, think about these things" (Phil 4:8).

Finally, we must accept our role, fulfill our responsibilities, and take charge of matters here on this earth. Christian participation in political, business, and educational areas of life is essential. We have both a right and an obligation to make crucial decisions. It's unfortunate that many thoughtful people hesitate to act because they don't understand the dilemma of God's sovereign purposes versus our freedom of will. They accuse ambitious people of playing God when they attempt new and different experiments. We need to realize there is a vast difference between foreknowledge and foreordination. I may know how a movie is going to end because I have read the book, but that doesn't mean I make the movie end in that particular way. I only know it because that is, in fact, the way the people who lived it and recorded it chose to act. Likewise, God merely sees the total picture in advance. He doesn't predestine that things will end in that exact way by imposing his will.

A casino is set up so the house wins overall, even though it may lose in specific instances. Likewise, God's purposes will win overall. Ultimate success is certain! Final victory is guaranteed! God's moral system is set up so evil negates and destroys itself and good affirms and enhances itself. Specific persons or groups can fail if they don't see fit to align themselves with truth and reality, but the movement itself will survive and triumph because truth is indestructible, goodness is invincible, and love is eternal.

Christians are expected to discover and bring in the kingdom, and that is happening. Humanitarian organizations and scientific discoveries are improving life. Boundaries are disappearing as methods of transportation become more efficient. The world is getting smaller as communication becomes almost instantaneous. The kingdom is escaping from its ecclesiastic jail cell, and its influence is touching the world. God, who is righteous, wants the best for us, and the best over the long term is human autonomy.

If some impending cataclysm must occur to overturn physical laws and miraculously destroy God's carefully nurtured creation, then that's not a positive outcome! If some supernatural force must swoop down and bail us out of our predicament and impose a mystical kingdom, then the whole marvelous spiritual/human experience called life has been a failure. Those who believe this are mistaken. God is not the author of defeat!

The doctrine of a physical second coming must be reinterpreted because it destroys God's creation, nullifies human achievement, and contradicts Jesus's promise of being with us always.

Conclusion

Twenty-first-century Christianity as we know it is becoming obsolete. Our assets are being appropriated by other organizations. We are being left behind as kingdom growth continues all around us. Often, the progress actually seems to be in spite of us instead of because of us. Many churches and congregations have gotten stuck on a few irrational traditional creeds and forgotten their purpose.

The theme of Christianity and the doctrinal approach and the priorities of Jesus have all been perverted by orthodox debris. Unfortunately, the complete reorientation we need will be difficult to achieve. Superimposing new concepts on a framework of old dogmas is almost impossible, and doubly so in the area of religion. That's why Jesus advised a drastic reinterpretation of the gospel (e.g., see Mark 2:22).

It's possible for worship to become so enmeshed in centuries of custom and so embedded in layers of tradition that to even mention divergent views or modified language seems sacrilegious. Tampering with holy things has always been considered taboo.

Jesus faced this in his day, and Christians who try to adapt the gospel to modern culture face it today. Since truth cannot be destroyed, contradictory ideas should be welcomed. People who repress different interpretations and fear an open forum are usually those who are unsure of their own faith. The ones who have real and solid faith won't need to deny freedom of expression.

We must analyze our beliefs and evaluate our doctrines:

1. If a doctrine adheres to traditional commandments and prohibitions rather than accepting new information and factual evidence, it's not valid! Therefore, the doctrine of scriptural inerrancy is not valid.

2. If a doctrine demands blind obedience and submission rather than encouraging autonomy and thoughtful responses, it's not valid! Therefore, the doctrine of divine sovereignty is not valid.

3. If a doctrine presents complicated and confusing concepts rather than giving simple and understandable explanations, it's not valid! Therefore, the doctrine of the Trinity is not valid.

4, If a doctrine requires formal creeds and rituals rather than emphasizing compassion and moral principles, it's not valid. Therefore, the doctrine of the vicarious atonement is not valid.

5. If a doctrine values inconsistent and uncertain expectations rather than relying on practical and realistic consequences, it's not valid. Therefore, the doctrine of supernatural miracles is not valid.

6. If a doctrine depicts a vindictive and ruthless God rather than a loving and truthful God, it's not valid. Therefore, the doctrine of a literal hell is not valid.

7. If a doctrine promotes fanciful and mystical occurrences rather than rewarding human initiative, it's not valid. Therefore, the doctrine of a physical second coming is not valid.

God created us in his image. He expects us to be thinkers as well as believers! To be productive in a scientific and technologically savvy world, we must use our intellectual faculties. Unless the doctrines we teach are reasonable, realistic, and responsible, we'll always end up in a knothole.

www.ingramcontent.com/pod-product-compliance
Lightning Source LLC
Chambersburg PA
CBHW071009160426
43193CB00012B/1986